Nov:

Trevor,

A very Happy Birthday.

love

David, Ted, Chad & Angus.

TRUCKS

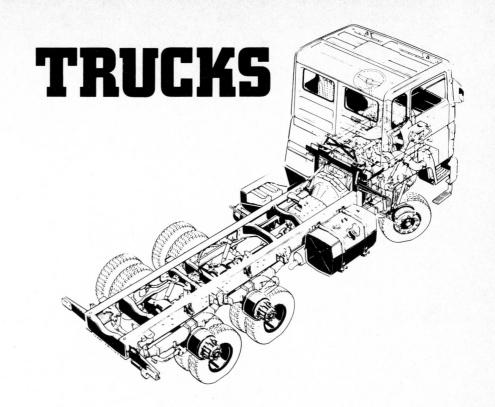

TRUCKS

Alan Thomas

HAMLYN
London·New York·Sydney·Toronto

The publishers are grateful to the following individuals and organisations for the illustrations in this book:

Bill Godwin; David Hodges; Leigh Jones; *Motor Transport*; Ian Muggeridge; Alan Thomas; Fred Weston; and all the manufacturers both past and present without whom this book would not have been possible.

Published by The Hamlyn Publishing Group Limited
London · New York · Sydney· Toronto
Astronaut House, Feltham, Middlesex, England

ISBN 0 600 38802 6
Phototypeset by Tradespools Limited, Frome, Somerset
Printed in Italy

CONTENTS

INTRODUCTION

Lorries share our roads and towns and, regrettably, intrude in unwelcome ways upon our lives. But almost everyone, every day, depends upon lorries. They bring our food and clothing, bricks and mortar, fuel and furniture. It is hard to imagine a domestic, social or industrial occupation that does not depend in some way upon lorries. Yet to most people road transport is a closed – almost secret – industry, something to be regarded with suspicion and distrust.

That is a great pity, for road transport contains much that is intrinsically interesting. This book is an attempt to convey some of that interest: it does not concentrate solely upon the vehicles, as so many transport publications do, but sets them in their historic and operational perspective. Nor does it concentrate on any single country, although the more prosperous nations of the world have naturally led the development of a transport mode which has done so much to foster that prosperity. Some technicalities are unavoidable when discussing a technical subject, but anyone with the slightest notion of how the family motor car works will have no difficulty in following the story of how commercial vehicles evolved from primitivism to the present day.

A.T.

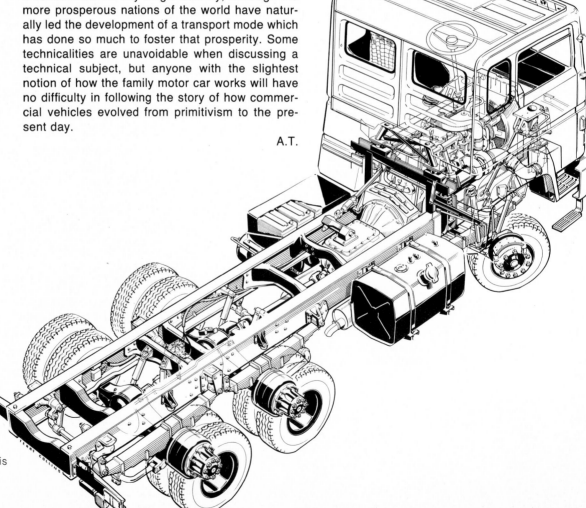

The Ford Transcontinental is representative of the multinational co-operation that forms such a major aspect of modern road transport.

EARLY YEARS

So clear is the connection between transport and the rest of industry and commerce that it is hardly possible to consider their development separately. Without trade there is no need for transport: without transport of some kind there can be no trade. The 'Third-World' peasant with his ox cart full of vegetables is essentially no different from the wholesale supplier trucking tonnes of luxury goods to Maceys of New York or Harrods of London.

Not so long ago, when communities were small and individual expectancies and ambitions hardly extended beyond subsistence, a high degree of self-sufficiency kept demands for inland transport to a level where pack horses were perfectly able to manage. Fuelling was easy and cheap, no roads – at most a few tracks – were required, and pannier baskets could carry to even the remotest community all the goods that local craftsmen could not make for themselves.

The explosion of industrial activity during the second half of the eighteenth century is capable of several interpretations, but one thing is clear: it was a peculiarly British, almost English, phenomenon. Nowhere else in the world combined the essential factors of need, resources and will. Just as other nations discovered a need for guns and pumps, nails and chains, pots and pans, the English harnessed their coal and iron with a singleminded determination and a fierce commercial intent unequalled anywhere before or since.

Deep-sea shipping came first, rapidly followed by rivers made navigable to commercially viable craft. Then came the artificial canal system – the first flowering of British civil engineering skills. Water transport (maritime and inland) was and is cheap transport. More important, it can easily carry low-value bulk goods and heavy cargoes. Unfortunately, it is also slow. Within reason, the length of time spent in transit by a consignment of coal, or lime, or pig-iron, or bricks, is not of particular moment. People and correspondence are another matter: as the eighteenth century drew to an end, Europeans still took days to travel by road, even between major towns; where possible, they travelled by water. No prudent person travelled at all unless it was absolutely necessary, and world travel of any kind was a rare and dangerous adventure.

Again, the English took the initiative. Prompted by the wisdom of keeping the further-flung parts of the newly United Kingdom in touch with London, they built superb new roads, with fine well-drained

surfaces, and with bridges instead of fords and ferries. Similar political logic had once prompted the Romans to build their empire-unifying network of roads, and Napoleon in his day to lay down the French Routes Nationales.

The new British road system expanded rapidly: by 1830 a network of splendid highways linked every town of any importance. As it grew, so did a comprehensive state-monopoly postal system, with an integral premium-charge passenger service.

Most of the British canal system suffered from being the pioneer of its kind: the waterways were too narrow, and the boats had insufficient capacity to withstand rail and motor lorry competition. Even so they were a long time dying.

7

Private enterprise soon joined in, providing frequent inter-urban coaches for those who could afford the fares. Inevitably, chains of hostelries capable of providing a high degree of comfort for men and horses grew up: the whole became a reliable communications system, finely tuned to the needs of the newly-emerging industrialists and businessmen. Bulk goods continued to travel by water, but the new roads made it possible to refine goods wagon construction. Vehicles became lighter, more efficient and generally better adapted to fetch and carry for old and new industries alike.

In a sense, all these forms of transport represented the final phase of man's dependence on natural forces: less than ten years after the world's first all-steam powered railway – the Liverpool and Manchester – began operations, the canals were forgotten and silting, while the roads deteriorated into little more than local byways. Within days of any new railway opening, the mail and stage coaches were withdrawn and the great inns and posting houses closed their stables and dining rooms. Thousands of coachmen, ostlers and servants were thrown into penury. Steam ruled supreme. Where a few years before, a rich man would have had to spend days on a difficult and uncomfortable journey, working class excursionists in their hundreds could now make a day trip of it at a cost of pennies. It was, in its way, a revolution more sudden and profound than any other in the history of mankind. It spread, too, in a manner more complete than any other revolution: by the end of the nineteenth century no nation of any significance had escaped the Railway Revolution.

As with passengers, so with freight. Every newly-made junction on the railways opened another through route for goods. Fresh foodstuffs became available everywhere. Tradesmen whose horizons had for generations been limited to serving customers within walking or horseback distance found vast new markets opening for them. Coal and iron,

the very stuff of this great industrial revolution, became cheap and plentiful everywhere.

But railways, although seemingly all-pervading, could not reach every village and hamlet; even from the earliest days their rigid routeing, which would ultimately prove a fatal weakness, left opportunities for the apparently redundant roads. To be sure, the nearest station yard was the furthest extent of most road journeys, but as the nineteenth century wore on, the inflexibility of rail transport forced the development, particularly in industrial towns, of sophisticated networks of freight and parcel collection and delivery. While horses provided the motive power there could be no significant advances in vehicle design, but speeds in city streets were little different then to rates of progress in congested thoroughfares now, and the whole formed a sizeable reservoir of experience in such road freight operating matters as vehicle scheduling, costs and charges, and staffing, all of which would prove useful later on.

Of the many factors contributing to the decline of railways in most industrialised countries, route inflexibility was undoubtedly one of the most intractable. Less obvious was the understandable tendency among the original railway builders to serve those areas which readily generated the most traffic. All too often that traffic later dwindled. Coal and iron ore beds became worked out, ships outgrew old docks, manufacturing concerns merged, faded or moved away. But the railway branch or siding remained, unused. Worse still, many trunk rail routes, which were seldom decided with any logical national plan in mind, became irrelevant. As more and more entirely new industries appeared on the scene, it became imperative for another, quite different mode of transport to evolve – the mechanically propelled road vehicle.

It had nearly happened once before: a handful of enthusiasts built a few steam powered carriages even before Victoria ascended the British throne.

Urban congestion is no new phenomenon, and it is clear from this turn of the century picture of The Bank, in London, that goods vehicles were common in horse days. Most of these vans and wagons would be connecting railway stations, or making local deliveries.

Most were British, lured on by those splendid roads and the dream of riches to be gained if mechanical traction could somehow be made to supplant horse-drawn coaches. The pioneers were encouraged by the ready availability of materials and tools. Experimenters were at work elsewhere, too – in France and Germany and even in America. If these pioneers were alive today, it has been said, they would probably make model steam locomotives for a hobby, and they would certainly tinker with the family car. In any event, their efforts all came to nought: the steam carriage builders had still to establish their credibility by producing vehicles capable of continuous work when the steam railway arrived, and the railway was so perfectly attuned to the needs of the time that nothing could stand in its way. By 1840 the steam carriage was dead and forgotten, although it is worth observing that almost no one ever showed interest in freight-carrying road steamers; it was essentially the railway that generated inland freight movement on a wholesale scale.

Broadly, the railway domination of inland transport lasted until the end of the nineteenth century. Alternatives certainly came into being, but none could do more than chip at the monolith of rail. These puny assailants were not irrelevant, however. Their attacks were insidious, and although no one, least of all their promoters and enthusiasts, realised it at the time, they were changing national attitudes. Urban steam tramways, for example, led townsfolk to see that something like door to door transport could be had cheaply and independently of both railway and horse. The tram also sold the idea of large machines rolling through town streets, and although steam tramways (much opposed by most communities) were never numerous, they certainly prepared the way for public acceptance of their legitimate successors, the electric tramway and the motor bus. These two modes of transport

There was no lack of steam carriage builders during the first three decades of the nineteenth century: almost to a man, however, they were thoroughly unsuccessful. The materials and technology of the day were simply inadequate. One of the very few steamers built expressly for goods was this 3 tonnes capacity van of 1823, by Julius Griffith of London. High hopes were voiced – but it, too, lumbered off into limbo.

Steam trams – actually small locomotives hauling one or more trailers – were never very common, but they were sufficiently widespread and useful to accustom townspeople to the idea of mechanical vehicles running through streets. Burnley was one of several industrial British towns to rely on steam trams, but other countries used similar combinations.

Larger trams were used for heavy transport but most users found that a pair of horses was as much as could be conveniently handled in city streets. Bus horses were expensive and shortlived: there was every incentive for large bus companies to take up the new motors, and to persevere with them.

involved in passenger carrying. Distances travelled by goods of all kinds on road vehicles were short, and since labour was universally cheap, the cost of manhandling goods from road to rail and back again seemed unimportant. On the other hand, travellers have never relished multi-vehicle journeys and long walks. As soon as a town expanded to a diameter of more than a couple of kilometres, the incentive to provide some kind of bus – and to ride in it – became irresistable.

The essence of any bus service is regularity, running at stated times over recognised routes. When buses were horse-drawn, expenses were high: no less than 12 animals were required to horse a typical bus in the 1890s (allowing for rest days and sickness) and their average working life in harness was no more than four or five years. Carrying capacities were low: few buses seated more than 26 passengers, because that was as many as a pair-horse team could manage. A larger team would have been too unwieldy in traffic.

This long-standing combination of circumstances suited the development of motor vehicles as replacements on established services. Predictable load factors gave a good indication of income (if not of unexpected and usually daunting expenses) while fixed routes and timetables meant that repair crews knew where to look for missing vehicles. These first motorised commercial vehicles were, almost without exception, financial disasters, but mechanical development went ahead so quickly that promoters hardly had time to lose courage and revert to horses. Whatever their shortcomings, the early engineering pioneers learned quickly and the chassis they produced were not only capable of carrying omnibus bodywork. They could also be used as lorries.

ruined the railway monopoly of short-distance travel and eventually led to the wholesale closure of suburban and rural stations and of branch lines – with, of course, a simultaneous reduction in rail facilities for the handling of goods.

What trams and buses did for public transport the bicycle did for the individual, who could thereby indulge his urge to wander free of fancy and company timetables. It all helped undermine the blind acceptance by earlier generations of the unassailable monopoly of rail.

At the time it was inevitable that the development of successful mechanical road transport should be in the hands of engineers and businessmen

While the early buses were, by and large, used to supplant horse-drawn vehicles, their goods-carrying brethren tended to become trail-blazers, open-

ing up inter-urban routes that had seen no direct freight services since the wagons of 70 years before. Nor was it only operational flexibility that made these earliest truck services appealing to users: after all, the railways were providing a very effective network of services and had done so for decades. Instead, it rapidly dawned on potential customers – as it has done ever since – that door to door transport meant greater security for consignments and hardly any breakages; cargoes could be loaded by the owner's employees, be under the eye of one man during the journey, and be off-loaded by the customer. No longer had fragile and valuable products to be consigned, perforce, to the risks of pilfering, damage, and delay inseparable from any large and impersonal transport monopoly. Incredibly, those earliest motor lorries – small, slow, noisy, and seemingly for ever breaking down – could outperform the lordly railway. Such vehicles, owned by men anxious and willing to please, were cheap to hire, too: in fact, from the customer's point of view, they were efficient! The discovery was made simultaneously throughout Europe and North America, and in the countries which reflected European influence – South Africa, Australia, New Zealand, the French and German territories of the Far East and Africa, and in parts of South America.

Conditions in these far-flung places were difficult, even by the standards of road transport in the home countries. By happy coincidence, however, pioneering, the opening up of new lands, and warfare are often – from the transport point of view – very similar activities. As many manufacturers began to offer 'Colonial' versions of their chassis, the military men of Europe, eyeing each other during those sunny but uneasy years before

1914, began to explore the possibilities of mechanical transport. Cavalry and infantry were most certainly the pride of every nation, but the wars of centuries past had unfailingly shown that the weakest link in sustaining or defending an attack was almost invariably the supply of food and ammunition to front-line troops. During the last decade of peace before 1914, generals became uncomfortably aware of the prospect of a rail-transported and fast-moving war. Motor transport was widely seen as an alternative way of replacing slow-moving, quick-tiring, provender- and water-consuming horse-drawn baggage trains with something very much better. The military men were not nearly so blind as history commonly relates, wilfully or otherwise, to the imminence of mechanical transport in war.

There was a brief flirtation in a few countries, notably Britain and Germany, with what were termed heavy oil tractors for army and colonial use. In many ways these machines resembled something between small steam traction engines and the kind of four-wheeled agricultural tractors that became popular from the 1920s onwards. The heavy oil was generally spark-ignited paraffin or kerosene, and the tractors were mainly intended to haul two or three horse-style wagons, often with the added advantage of an engine-driven winch to aid recovery when a less than usually adequate road collapsed. But tractors and trailers were a dead end in road transport development: they could never equal the speed or convenience of separate load-carrying vehicles, and their vogue was largely over by the time war erupted in 1914.

Vehicle trials were held in plenty, with maker pitched against maker, and factory drivers cursing

In the years before motor lorries proved their potential for war, heavy steam locomotives showed how useful mechanical traction could be. These Fowlers, on trials, went to help in the Boer War during 1900, where they showed one weakness of steam: the difficulty in arranging suitable fuel supplies. They were converted to oil-burners.

Opposite:
A goods transshipment dock on the Canadian National Railway. The expense and wasted time is self-evident, yet there is no alternative when goods are carried by rail. Inevitably, users soon realise that one lorry can take their consignments all the way, with no need to transfer from lorry to train and back again.

On manoeuvres. A machine gun company with its weapons on a borrowed civilian lorry *(top)*. Exercises of this kind across Europe proved beyond doubt that war, when it came again, would be the first mechanised conflict in history. Some makers, even before 1910, were designing machines expressly for military use. Broom and Wade, now a world-famous maker of air compressor equipment, concentrated for some years on paraffin fuelled internal combustion tractors suitable for cross-country work *(above)*.

as they coaxed their narrow-tyred, underpowered and almost brakeless charges across muddy ravines and hills as steep as roofs on some deserted heath. The army commanders stood superciliously by, boots and leatherwork glistening in the sun, although they too were learning quickly. One far-reaching result was the subvention schemes, instituted by several governments. The idea was simple: civilian owners of suitable vehicles who undertook to keep them in good condition received regular payments from the state. In return, their vehicles had to be available at short notice in the event of national emergency. There may have been something a little absurd about long lines of vans on prewar manoeuvres bearing the liveries and names of respectable haberdashers and provision merchants, but the intent and effect were both deadly serious: mechanisation on a scale hitherto undreamed of was coming to the business of war.

There were interesting differences in the way nations organised their subvention schemes. Railbound Germany, one of the first to put such matters on a formal basis, realised early on that it had virtually no civilian road transport industry at all, and that its two or three makers of heavy vehicles exported most of their production. The government thereupon instituted a plan under which it paid something approaching half the original cost of vehicles designed and built to stringent requirements, and which were bought by private users. Quite apart from any other consideration, this move effectively founded the German road transport industry.

France, appropriately, adopted a *laissez-faire* approach, and while large sums of money were paid out, the overall results were less satisfactory in that almost any vehicle capable of meeting performance criteria was deemed eligible. Although individual units were perfectly adequate, the effect was to create a large and motley fleet likely to become a maintenance nightmare. An incidental curiosity was a long-lasting predeliction of the French authorities, in the face of industry opposition, for steel tyres, even on vehicles capable of 30km/h – a quirk which was abandoned only a year or so before the First World War broke out. The French also favoured designs in which the cab was positioned over the engine.

Austria adopted a scheme much in line with the German plan, for the Austrian Empire at that time contained a number of heavy vehicle makers. Russia, on the other hand, realised to its dismay during an early series of trials that all the vehicles on show were imported, that there were few men able to handle them, and that the country had virtually no roads suitable for heavy motor traffic.

One of the last deliberate subsidy schemes to be instituted by a government was that of the Japanese in 1918. At that time, it was reckoned that Japan possessed a grand total of only 4,000 motors, and sizeable sums of money were therefore offered as an inducement to prospective users. So successful was the plan that it led to lorry-making factories being built.

Perhaps the only modern survivor of the classic subvention schemes is run in Switzerland, and even there few vehicles are nowadays involved.

Having no doubt learned a great deal, not only from its own experience but from that of others (for there were few apparent attempts by anyone at imposing secrecy), Britain adopted a plan which served the home country and its empire very well indeed between 1914 and 1918 – and for a decade after that. The military authorities in London laid down basic specifications for future candidates for their bounty: although some details were closely specified, including the arrangements of driving controls and a ban on chain final drive, much was

left to the many manufacturers who decided to produce suitable vehicles. The results all bore a marked external resemblance to each other but apart from some bearings, wheels, radiators, and bodywork, components were not interchangeable.

Thus it would appear that a fundamental element in any campaign to establish a national and truly universal transport fleet was lost, and in one sense it was. More important by far, however, was the confidence engendered by these 'government-approved' designs, and the resulting impetus given to potential vehicle owners to buy them. Demand from the civilian market increased, production rose, buyers got machines they felt they could trust, the terms of the subsidy agreement had the effect of keeping maintenance standards to a satisfactory level and the military gained access to a large pool of reliable vehicles at a comparatively low cost. So good were these chassis that, when the war was over, they became the standard British heavy petrol lorries of the 1920s. A handful, albeit heavily modified, even lingered on into the 1940s and 1950s.

Meanwhile the United States Army, secure in its geographical and political isolation, made only desultory attempts to replace its horse-drawn buggies with 1·5 tonne capacity motor trucks. Until, that is, the Mexican War, when the American authorities realised the advantages of motor traction to an army at war. By the time the USA joined the First World War in 1917, plans were in hand for the production of huge fleets of highly standardised vehicles, built up from components and sub-assemblies from many factories, and in which an engine or gearbox by one maker could be replaced by units made elsewhere.

Although it did not become clear for another 20 years, lorry design had already settled into its definitive form by this time. The engine was at the front and drove the rear wheels through some form of variable speed reduction gearing. A separate chassis frame accommodated all the mechanical components, and carried separate bodywork adapted to suit the cargoes envisaged.

Another profound decision had also been made: lorries would be powered by internal combustion

By 1920 Europe was littered with thousands of motor vehicles left behind by the armies. Many were more or less fit for use and, with their army-trained drivers, formed the foundation of the modern road transport industry. Leyland took the unique step of buying back a great many of the 'subvention' vehicles it had made and reconditioning them in the factory *(below)* for resale on the civilian market.

13

When petrol was scarce, uncertain of quality, and expensive there was an understandable desire to use paraffin — readily available for domestic lighting and heating. At much the same time, displaced horses were leaving many usable wagons behind them, so a few makers tried to popularise paraffin-engined tractors. These hovered in an uncertain market between agriculture and the military, and soon disappeared. This Marshall was built about 1905.

engines of one kind or another and would be fuelled by liquid, mineral oil-based products. In a way, this was strange, for in 1900 (as good a date as any from which to trace the development of commercial road transport in the modern sense) oil technology was young and primitive and known fuel reserves were limited. On the other hand, the only practicable alternative form of power – steam – had reached a high level of technical development, was widely understood, and had already been demonstrated by several makers as an effective source of power for road vehicles. But traditional steam engines required high standards of competence from their human attendants. For road work, where operating conditions change by the minute and almost by the metre, skills had to be higher still, and there was a limited reserve of men willing and able to undertake the long hours and hard work that driving a road steamer entailed. Another problem, just as difficult in many parts of the world, was the inavailability of suitable coal and coke. Many things can be burned to heat water, but the taxing conditions of road traction require specialised fuels that were not generally available. Finding suitable and adequate water supplies is also more difficult than it might at first appear.

The petrol (occasionally paraffin) engine, on the other hand, could be driven by anyone capable of co-ordinating hand and foot movements. Provided it kept running, engine output was predictable; even though the early gearboxes and clutches would be considered impossible by most modern drivers, there was no boiler to tend, no water to find, and no coal to carry. Liquid fuels were certainly of poor and variable quality but they contained more energy for volume or weight than solid fuels. These were big advantages, and petrol vehicle development went ahead so rapidly that steam was soon outdistanced: the truth of the matter was

that steam power in all its manifestations had already reached a high and wide plateau of evolution. Lighter materials, welding, and pneumatic tyres were able, in later years, to take it a little further in road transport, but not much.

Internal combustion, on the other hand, had enormous and visible potential for development. Perhaps the most significant nail in the coffin of steam traction for use on common roads was its rejection by military authorities. Comparing the nimble if crude petrol lorries on those pre-1914 trials with the lumbering steamers, the choice must have seemed clear even then. When war came, the decision was fully justified as thousands of easily mass-produced petrol lorries went into battle. Steamers were there, too, but they were comparatively few in number and worked well back from the front lines. If nothing else, the glow from their fireboxes was too good a target for enemy gunners.

The First World War certainly had a profound effect on both vehicle design and manufacturing methods. The petrol-engined chassis of 1920 may have looked much the same as their predecessors of 1910, but they were actually very different. The biggest single improvement lay in the materials: not only were there advantages in making special heat-resistant steels suitable for engine components, but fuels had been much improved, rubber for tyres was vastly better than anything available before the war; the huge quantities of chassis required for the war effort by every country had made it worthwhile to build giant presses capable of stamping out major items like chassis frame members; casting techniques and metals for things like engine cylinder blocks and gearboxes became much improved and so too were the theories of gear cutting and lubrication.

The war had another profound effect on the subsequent peace with the flood of cheap 'surplus' vehicles, and of qualified mechanics and drivers released on to civilian markets. In the absence of almost any relevant legislation the outcome was inevitable, and by the very early 1920s hordes of hard-working and determined young men were vying with each other for the chance to carry goods and passengers. Not a few also turned skills acquired in the armed services to good account in the field of vehicle repair and maintenance.

Rates were low and rewards slim, for although competition is a fine thing it is easily overdone, and while customers had little to cavil at in the levels of service they were offered, it was often at the expense of over-long working hours for drivers, poor pay, and profit levels too low to replace vehicles or maintain them properly; only the subsequent formation of large operating groups alleviated these problems. More to the point, however, a decade of competition at this ferocious level was quite beyond the ability of any railway to tackle.

Governments inevitably took a hand and began to frame a web of laws and regulations that has steadily thickened from that day to this. Licensing systems, under which an aspiring operator had to prove the need for any route or service he wished to offer, became common. Working hours and pay were regulated, and government engineers, usually in close collaboration with the manufacturing side of the industry, laid down precise and uniformly applied stipulations about such basic matters as overall dimensions, weights, braking, lighting and steering. All of this came none too soon: it was one thing to contemplate a small, ill-maintained truck creeping along at 16–20km/h over dusty, stony roads, its work-exhausted driver peering over the old sack that served to protect him in the otherwise completely open cab; it was quite another prospect to face lorries with two or three times the capacity and perhaps four times the speed running unchecked for hundreds of kilometres over the smoothly surfaced main roads that were criss-crossing every country of any importance.

The change from unregulated primitivism in road freight transport was more or less complete by 1930 in most developed parts of the world. This synchronism is not altogether surprising, for the final years of the 1920s were another period in which heavy motor vehicle design made major advances, and the pressures of economics during those worldwide slump years compelled chassis makers to look very closely indeed at their buying and selling practices. Motor vehicles readily lend themselves to the process of unit construction, in which individual components are put together to form sub-assemblies that are only later married up to form complete machines. The degree of specialisation that can be brought to bear on each component is considerable and production in vast quantities keeps prices low. No chassis manufacturer makes his own rubber tyres; electrics are almost invariably bought in, as are glass, bearings, friction materials, and many castings and forgings. Since quality and price depend on quantity production, makers of such items had a great incentive to find new markets among vehicle builders outside their home countries. Inevitably, the complexity of items offered by specialist suppliers increased: soon engines, gearboxes, axles and even body pressings were being traded internationally.

By the early 1930s, both chassis and component manufacturers were setting up complete assembly plants overseas. It was a development pioneered by American companies, who saw that their designs, capable of coping with poor roads, long

It is a moot point whether the vehicle was too heavy for the bridge, or the bridge not strong enough for the truck. An enormous and sustained effort – and expense – had to be made in recently and newly settled countries to provide road systems capable of carrying the unprecedented motor vehicle.

American motor manufacturers had a large enough market to force them into mass production of light and medium weight trucks long before most other countries. Cheap, good-looking, and reliable products like this Ford of the 1930s proved to be formidable competition for less effective makers.

Provided the radius of operation is no more than about 5 km horses can, even now, prove economically attractive. It was not until the cheap, American inspired, 2–3 tonne tippers became generally available that these one-horse carts finally faded away from general use.

distances and extremes of climate at home would be well able to survive conditions in most other parts of the world. They had an even greater advantage: American manufacturing methods, spurred on by wholesale demand and by the limitations imposed by a largely unskilled workforce, could produce vehicles at a speed and price unrivalled anywhere else. Detroit was mass-producing good-value trucks when the techniques were still hardly understood even by the popular car manufacturers in Europe.

These invaders, whether imported whole or home-assembled, rapidly became a major factor in short-distance road transport in most parts of the world. They lacked longevity – initially at least – and thereby left ample markets for more traditional exponents of hand-crafted engineering in larger capacity vehicles and for those users willing to pay for nicely made light and medium chassis. But the mass-producers, backed by what were to all intents and purposes limitless funds, kept expanding. Each new range of products, always competitively priced, was more durable and generally more acceptable that its predecessors; gradually, as market demands intensified, carrying capacities increased. Now, 40 years on, the handful of mass-production American giants, together with the very few European and Japanese concerns that have seriously sought to match them, have achieved domination in world markets. Dozens of lesser rivals have perished along the way.

Rapid and steady improvements to vehicle design led, naturally enough, to equally rapid advances in the scope and quality of the services that could be offered by lorry operators. Indeed, 'Service' became the slogan of the industry. Faster lorries, better brakes and lighting and, above all, pneumatic tyres, meant that customers could rely on railway-like speed and accuracy in timekeeping. Overnight journeys soon produced a degree of service that could not be equalled: goods collected just before a factory closed for the day, or loaded overnight, were delivered to the customer as he opened his business next morning. The low unit cost of capital equipment (for lorries were comparatively cheap to buy until quite recent years) meant that a vehicle could be specially tailored to suit any commodity: if the job was sufficiently lucrative, special bodywork – even special chassis – could be made.

As vehicles and roads improved, both makers and users began to cast speculative eyes on even more distant places. For a horse-drawn wagon, 20 km or so comprised a fair day's work; even the earliest motors could double, treble, quadruple that, and by the 1930s the speed and reliability of vehicles had become hardly relevant in determining the amount of work that could be handled. Now it was the endurance of drivers that formed the limiting factor, and here too parameters began to stretch, with cabs becoming roomier and quieter, seats and controls ergonomically designed to minimise fatigue, and – above all – wide, fast, purpose-made roads along which lorries can now speed for hour after hour at average rates that the sports cars of 50 years ago could hardly equal, and which come perilously close to the best possible performances of railway freight trains.

Land frontiers between nations soon lost any operational significance, the chief hindrances to international traffic being, as in so many other things, the obstructive manoeuvrings of politicians. Even the sea began to lose its old importance. Until the 1950s any heavy vehicle that went aboard ship had to be lifted there by crane; in all likelihood it had been sold to an export market and was unlikely to make a return journey. But then one or two enterprising ferry operators on the busiest and shortest of sea crossings began to provide ships adapted for roll-on/roll-off (ro-ro) loading. Within a very few years international freight traffic was transformed, as the trickle of lorries going ro-ro became a flood. New ports came into being and old ones withered as the network of routes and services provided by road transport grew ever more comprehensive. It is still growing and there are no signs that this growth is even nearing its peak.

If 'Service' became the slogan of the industry, 'Service or Die' might well have been adopted by many of the men engaged in it, for road transport is and always has been an occupation for small, independently-minded businessmen: almost anyone can buy a lorry and begin trading. Thousands have done so and many have failed, but it is remarkable that in every free-economy state the overwhelming proportion of road transport is supplied by small fleets of vehicles. Where attempts have been made to monopolise the industry, with either private or state capital, the resulting inefficiency has caused discontented customers to move away and find other solutions to their needs. Sometimes, particularly in Britain, they have even been lured into buying and running lorries themselves. Times may be changing for these fleets, however: in the past large industrial or trading concerns could regard lorries and drivers as low-cost items – something of a convenient adjunct to the main business rather than a serious expense. Such own-account operations were traditionally less cost-effective and less used than lorries which plied for hire.

Now the complexity and stringency of transport law, combined with elaborate and expensive vehicles and much enhanced wages and living standards for transport workers, are persuading fleet owners that possession is more trouble than it is worth – yet they still want detailed control over the vehicles. Increasingly the solution is for a professional transport concern to provide (under long-term contract) a fleet of lorries and drivers tailored to the user's needs and to assume full responsibility for maintenance, staffing and ensuring that suitable reserves are always available. Quite often the agreement also includes the warehousing and distribution of the client's products. The practice of using rented rather than owned transport is spreading even to operators carrying for hire as they, too, find it difficult to justify the high capital outlay or debt-servicing charges required to finance the purchase of modern heavy vehicles. Instead, they turn to rental companies: trailer hire is already a very important business indeed, and every year companies renting out trucks report increases in their fleets and numbers of customers. Providing such financially orientated services is clearly something only the largest of transport companies can undertake, although each separate contract or hire usually comprises a relatively small operation.

International frontiers have only political significance for modern hauliers; even the sea is hardly an obstacle, for roll-on/roll-off ferries act almost as floating bridges. This Czechoslovakian-owned Skoda and its drawbar trailer worked regularly from Prague to London.

The great drawback to steam wagons was the need for a boiler: always heavy, usually large, and preferably able to convert water into steam quickly and cheaply. Several quite distinct forms of boiler were adopted, but only Yorkshire used a double-ended transversely mounted unit.

1914. 6 TON. YORKSHIRE.
THE CHART CARRYING Co.
BRASTED, KENT.
Telephone
BRASTED.
256.

MASS PRODUCTION AND STANDARDISATION

Stand for an hour or two by the side of a main road almost anywhere in the world and watch the great lorries roll by. Many will be articulated, with a tractor carrying the front end of a separate trailer; others will very likely be mounted on two or three axles (four or six wheels), carrying any of a dozen different kinds of bodywork holding any of a thousand different kinds of cargo. The identities of many chassis makers will soon become familiar, for most of them mount their names in large letters across the driving cabs of their products. Indeed, these well-displayed trademarks are usually the most clearly distinguishable thing about them, for each vehicle is much the same overall size as others of its class, and although there is certainly some stylistic variety between cabs old and new, those of any one generation are very much alike.

Really acute observers may soon recognise cab doors or other sheet metal pressings that clearly come from one supplier, or the unobtrusive little badges mounted on the front which imply that the power unit comes from one of the specialist engine makers. A certain similarity may even be noticed in the shape of wheel hubs, denoting that axles can also be brothers under the skin. In short, there is no denying that, whoever the builder, there is a very close resemblance between vehicles for specific on-highway purposes, no matter whose name adorns the overall result.

The main reason is clear enough: legal requirements are now all-pervading in virtually every country, and the burgeoning growth of both international vehicle sales and cross-frontier operations has compelled governments to adopt road transport laws which are essentially compatible with those of their neighbours. This uniformity has naturally been seized upon by most vehicle makers and their suppliers as a heaven-sent opportunity to rationalise products and thereby lengthen production runs. End-users are consoled by assurances that in losing variety they gain better value.

For many years, manufacturers capable of producing the parts they needed looked in disdain upon lesser firms who merely assembled bits produced by others. There is a great deal in the traditional argument that only by making everything itself can a company guarantee the quality of its products and be certain of complete compatibility between their component parts, but as usual the coin has another side. When development is rapid, as it has been throughout the history of road vehicles, designs and manufacturing methods must change rapidly. Either a factory must make heavy and repeated investments in new techniques and products, usually unjustified by the likely volume of sales, or it must stay with the obsolete, thereby losing ground to those that have gone ahead. Worse still, once a plant is committed to manufacture an engine, gearbox, or axle it has to go on, contriving as best it may to overcome any defects that show up in customers' hands. It is a remarkable fact that the demise of many once-famous makes followed the marketing of just one or two models containing ill-developed components: dubious engines in particular have had much to answer for.

While proud giants of the commercial vehicle building industry confidently pursue their idiosyncratic ways, there have always been sufficient outlets available in engineering generally to justify volume production by specialist component producers. There may not be a great deal of outward similarity between the equipment used by different industries but they all need gears, bearings, castings and fabrications, and the total market is sufficient to justify and pay for the research which makes advances in such technology generally available. Engines are a prime case: welding sets, boats, pumps, compressors, and road vehicles can all use a basic power unit modified to meet each purpose by easily-added and relatively cheap accessories. With gearboxes and axles, different ratios can be installed in outwardly similar casings, while identical final drive units can be used in long or short axle housings.

At a stroke, therefore, sub-assembly manufacturers have access to markets large enough to warrant volume production and their customers have access to several sources of reliable supplies, even though they may only require very small quantities. In more recent years the trend has accelerated, and there are now few chassis-building factories who do not offer at least some major assemblies made by others. It is safe to predict that when the present generation of commercial vehicle models, notably in western Europe, reaches the end of its useful life, own-sourcing will cease for all but the highest volume models, where in-house demand is so great that it justifies home production. The rest of the free world will then fall into line with America, which from the earliest days has very largely depended upon lorries built up entirely from parts made by independent suppliers.

For the end-users, assembled chassis can offer

Axles – bought in; brake components – bought in; chassis frame – supplied by a specialist; and so on, and so forth. In the beginning, most motor manufacturers made virtually all the components in their chassis. Specialist suppliers gradually proved they could produce parts better and cheaper and soon virtually all the components used by many makers originated elsewhere. Thornycroft assembled this four-axled machine; ultimately the firm took the final step so common among motor makers – it merged with rivals, then disappeared.

some real advantages. Operators in remote areas may well be less concerned with the nominal makes of their vehicles than with the engines that power them, for one engine supplier may well be better represented locally by sales and service depots than a rival concern. Not infrequently, a vehicle buyer already owns a fleet of cranes or other civil engineering plant, and wants to standardise his engines to simplify maintenance. He can now shop around several large and successful lorry makers for the best price and delivery, and still get the power unit of his choice.

An incidental advantage of the assembly system for chassis manufacturers is that although the big firms need sizeable design and production departments, a number of smaller ones can manage very well without. These enterprising concerns have identified market gaps – crevices, more usually – overlooked or disdained by the motor industry giants but which, with low operating overheads and a close awareness of customer needs, can be exploited by the smaller companies. Even the troublesome matter of finding suitable cabs to meet modern requirements is not insurmountable, given a little ingenuity and good will from the mass-producers. Many fire appliances, rough ground tippers, crane carriers, crash tenders and other specialised vehicles have come about because of teamwork between an understanding customer, an enterprising vehicle builder and the component makers.

Despite the advantages of specialisation in design and manufacture, all is not perfect, perhaps the biggest single drawback to volume production of components and chassis being a stifling of the spirit of adventure in design offices. No company whose profitability (and therefore existence)

Even the biggest companies have recourse to specialist suppliers. When Ford was looking for a larger engine capable of fitting under its D-series tilt cab it turned to Perkins – but insisted that the Ford name was cast into the rocker covers.

In its steam wagon days Fodens made almost everything itself, and with the notable exception of its power units carried the tradition forward into its diesel engined designs. Ultimately the company even made some engines. Nor have Fodens lacked the spirit of adventure, and this ingenious adaptation of its standard eight-wheeler of the 1960s deserved wider acceptance.

Variations on van bodywork
are legion, with many
different versions, each
tailored to meet specific
requirements. The Kromhout
(above), a product of one of
the very few Netherlands
lorry makers, shows the fast
disappearing but once
popular practice of making
the cab integral with the
body.

Many small communities
throughout the world now
depend upon mobile shops
for supplies of foodstuffs
and other domestic
requirements. The mid-
1950s Saurer *(right)*, is an
example of the 'mobile
market stall' kind of
bodywork: in less favourable
climates the travelling
shopkeepers offer a walk-
through version.

Climbing up and down to
many conventional cabs, if
often repeated, is an
exhausting business and
several makers have tried to
make working conditions for
delivery drivers easier by
adopting low level cabs.
One of the most successful
was the Albion division of
Leyland which produced the
Claymore *(far right)*. Sadly,
although its advantages
were real, demand did not
justify continuance.

A medium weight Dennis illustrates one reason why front-wheel drive has rarely been favoured for commercial vehicles. Independent suspension becomes very desirable, and the resulting complications in driving, steering, and braking the one pair of wheels are in the main best avoided.

Overtype or undertype. To modern eyes the choice facing the steam wagon buyer of old seems obvious, but one of the fascinations of steam is its endless subtleties, and users found good reasons to patronise both types until the very last days of commercial steam. Few makers made both types simultaneously, although allegiances sometimes changed, but Mann (right) was an almost entirely overtype concern while Leyland (below) stayed loyal to undertypes.

nise a steam wagon or tractor from a petrol machine while still 100 m away: even with eyes closed, the rattle of a chain final drive was a sound distinct from any other. And there was little difficulty in identifying the peculiarly oily exhaust smell emitted by sleeve-valve engines.

This diversity usually resulted from attempts to cure the failings of contemporary designs, and no part of the vehicle escaped experimentation. Whole concepts were challenged: even the almost universally accepted layout of the basic components was called into question by two or three firms brave or rash enough to undertake the task of convincing the world that front-wheel drive for heavy vehicles was a sensible and practicable idea.

While petrol-engined machinery was primitive of manufacture and wayward of performance, there were distinct advantages in replacing the horse directly by a small tractor, usually steam-powered (sometimes kerosene or petrol) in order to take advantage of the well-established technology and equipment available from makers of agricultural plant. It rapidly dawned on users that one tractor was able to service three trailers: one loading, one unloading, and one in transit. Although the passing of time has taken its toll of this satisfying symmetry, the principle still holds good to some degree even in this articulated age.

Steam tractors were, on the whole, highly stan-

depends upon widespread acceptance of its wares can risk the perils of spectacular innovation.

It was not always so. While the basic format of the commercial vehicle was established early, diversity of ideas ran rife among designers and engineers for many years. No patient investigation was needed to identify differences between makes and models in the early days; anyone could recog-

dardised: their years of novelty had been the 1860s and 1870s, when some very strange devices flowered briefly. By 1900, design had stabilised, and any subsequent changes were relatively minor and intended only to meet revised legislation. Although using the expertise already built up by tractors, however, steam wagon designers had no compunction in going their own way. Some adopted a layout reminiscent of an extended tractor, with a long locomotive-type boiler at the front, the engine on top and available body space extending to no more than half the overall length. The result was crude but almost unbreakable, a valuable attribute at the time (although in later years this worked against salesmen struggling to persuade operators to replace hoary veterans of maybe 20 or 25 years, which showed no signs of wearing out, with something more modern).

For the steam devotee who wanted to buy something a little more refined and offering a greater quantity of body space than the elementary overtype, there was the undertype which, as the name suggests, carried its power unit beneath the chassis. Since the usual form of boiler on undertypes was vertical, it took up little space and could be accommodated, with its fuel, in cabs not much larger than those of today. Largely because of this small boiler, however, undertypes demanded from their crews a more delicate touch than overtypes, but both attracted loyal if noisy support. The debate continues among the considerable numbers of people who still care about such things, three decades after the last steamers were made.

The temptation to find a less refined, and therefore less expensive, liquid fuel than petrol was there from the earliest days, but technical difficulties proved more than a match for the materials then available for the highly stressed components in engines. Compared even with contemporary petrol engines, the oilers, which generally used kerosene, had a more erratic performance and smelt nastier. In the less taxing environment of the stationary engine, oil and gas proved perfectly satisfactory until overtaken by the unbeatable versatility of centrally generated electricity. For road vehicles of the heavier types, petrol reigned almost unchallenged until toppled by the type of oiler now generally known as the diesel.

In common with passenger cars, nearly all attempts to depart from traditional engine design for heavy vehicles were doomed to failure, and the poppet valve, four-stroke cycle combination has proved remarkably durable. Even the basic layout has changed little and most engines are still mounted vertically in the chassis with mechanically operated valves, accessories driven from the front, and the drive taken from a flywheel at the back. Other designs, notably the two-stroke cycle, have been tried and even succeeded to some degree, while occasional forays into horizontally opposed or vee-formation cylinder layouts have also challenged the traditional in-line engine. Vees are currently enjoying some popularity, but most owners still prefer the mechanical simplicity of in-lines. For the first 30 years four cylinders – or two – were deemed enough, but as vehicle sizes and user expectations advanced, the increased power and smoothness obtainable from six cylinders soon banished the four to lighter tasks. Since then, despite frequent doubts, the performance of the straight six has been kept in line with what has been required of it. An incidental advantage of the straight six commercial engine is that its overall length can be nicely housed over the front wheels of normal-control vehicles, or under the cabs of forward-control layouts, without extending back into the useful load space. Moreover, it is short enough to fit across the frame at the rear of a bus, a considerable advantage to manufacturers of passenger service vehicles, who seek clear uncluttered chassis.

The most profound change so far in engine practice for larger commercial vehicles has undoubtedly been the near-total abandonment of

petrol in favour of oil for fuel. By the end of their development, big petrol engines were certainly reliable enough, and their smooth and silent running brought the refinement of large private cars to the lorries and buses of the 1930s. Their downfall was extravagance: when oilers came they brought with them fuel economy three or more times better than the petrol engines they so rapidly replaced.

The real advantage of steam traction is great flexibility. The conventional reciprocating steam engine – the only kind used in road vehicles – has the useful property of exerting its maximum effort at the instant it begins to move its load. Thus no clutch or gearbox is needed, and either no speed reduction is required at all between engine and wheels (as in most railway steam locomotives) or at most a simple one- or two-stage reduction is provided. The latter served most road steamers, where light, high-speed engines were desirable but road speeds were low.

Internal combustion engines, unfortunately, are far less accommodating, being capable of producing useful power only when running at high speeds – and a limited range of speeds, at that. The problem of devising some sort of clutch capable of coupling a fast running engine to the road wheels of

Clearly an old engine (in fact a Great War subvention Leyland) but equally clearly a conventional internal combustion engine. From then until now most motor vehicles have been powered by four- or six-cylinder vertical engines descended from ancestors of this kind. Even the diesels are very similar in layout, and while other vee and flat arrangements have their adherents the vertical seems likely to endure.

By the time the big petrol engine era was drawing to a close, half a century ago, the standards of performance and finish frequently equalled the best private car practice. In common with most of its kind this French-built Bernard relied on magneto ignition, and the appearance of the whole under-bonnet assembly should have done a great deal to instil pride of ownership.

Local legislative peculiarities often led to distinctive local types of vehicle, and for many years Britain was the home of rigid eight-wheelers, often hauling drawbar trailers.

Then the law changed and they went out of fashion for a few years; now they are back, but unlike the early 1950s Atkinson (above), which was a general haulage machine, most modern examples are used for tipper work.

A great contrast in style is the little Bedford (right), whose long bonnet and pressed steel cab were unashamedly styled to appeal to people who were car-minded. Many went to market gardeners and the like, although easy access through the bonnet to running gear in those pre-tilt cab days also made the type successful in 'third world' markets.

Looking inside a modern gearbox for a heavy vehicle does much to explain the apparent attractions of steam and electric power, which require no such heavy and expensive aids. Yet despite their complexity such gearboxes – this one is a Scania – are very reliable, and rarely cause trouble in service.

a heavy vehicle without either stalling the former or dislocating the bones of passengers in the latter was one that defeated engineers for many years. Standardisation of conventional plate clutches, using asbestos-based compounds as the friction material, is now all but complete for lorries, and is likely to remain so until automatic transmissions, which replace at once the ordinary clutch and gearbox, supplant them.

As it happens, the pressures which have led to the widespread introduction of automatic, or more commonly semi-automatic, transmissions in buses are largely absent from lorries. For one thing, few goods vehicles stop and start as often in their working lives as a bus, and not many lorries have more than half the lifespan of a passenger vehicle. Therefore there is less time for owners to amortise the much higher initial costs, together with the normally higher fuel consumption caused by internal losses in an automatic. Nevertheless, modern urban road conditions can easily make life almost

intolerable for heavy vehicles and their drivers, and there is a noticeable tendency for refuse collection trucks and the like to be equipped with automatic transmissions.

In this respect (as in so many others) heavy passenger vehicles took the lead in innovation, and most early development work on transmissions was aimed at improving the lot of the bus passenger. Quite apart from the clutch, both gearbox and final drive demanded much from the men who drove and maintained them. Gearboxes, on the whole, used the sliding engagement principle common in cars and known illuminatingly as the crash (or clash!) box. Much nicer altogether were epicyclic transmissions, which kept their gears permanently in mesh and where the ratios to be used were engaged by means of internal band-brakes. Years elapsed before such transmissions were of use in anything but lightweight vehicles and when they resurfaced it was as the preselector, which became common in larger bus fleets.

A Tilling-Stevens petrol electric. The handsome four-cylinder engine is direct-coupled to a generator which lies under the driver's feet. The generator is electrically connected to a motor. Speed was controlled by adjusting the connections in the motor and the engine speed, with a hand lever under the steering wheel and the usual accelerator pedal.

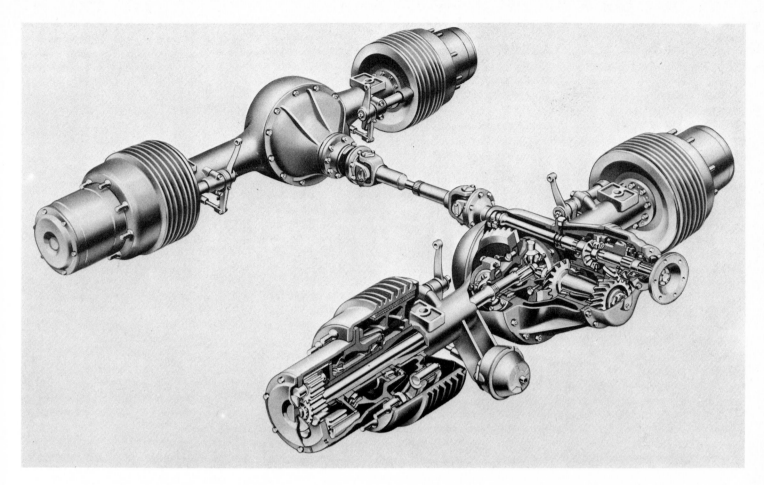

A measure of the desperation felt by operators over the inadequacy of contemporary transmissions was the time and effort devoted to developing petrol-electrics. This dead end on the road of commercial vehicle progress seems absurd now but it was taken seriously until the mid-1920s. A conventional engine mounted in the usual place was permanently connected by means of a short propeller shaft to a direct-current generator that lay in the place usually reserved for clutch and gearbox; the generator, in turn, was electrically linked to the motor, which drove the rear axle through another propeller shaft. This had one enormous advantage: no clutch, no gearbox, and therefore anyone capable of mastering a steering wheel could drive it. Petrol-electrics proved a godsend to many an ex-horse bus driver, and to those few urban lorry men whose employers were enlightened enough to buy them.

The technical and metallurgical paucity which led to so many unsatisfactory shifts in vehicle design during the early days showed up particularly clearly in final drives. Most builders overcame their problems by adopting side chains: fortunately roller chain of the kind still universal on bicycles was available in suitable sizes. It is a precision product, made to high and uniform standards of accuracy, and capable of withstanding wholly unreasonable amounts of abuse and ill-treatment: it was ideally matched to the purpose vehicle engineers had in mind. Although suitable for any kind of vehicle, it had two main drawbacks—high speeds, for either chains or vehicle, were impracticable and unwise, and it was almost impossible to protect the drive assembly from dust and water. Designers, having used chains for almost everything, therefore

sought to abandon them as soon as possible. Within a few years hardly any road vehicle of less than about 4 tonnes capacity—which included virtually all buses—was fitted with chains, most makers having adopted bevel gears (for chassis up to about 2·5 tonnes capacity) or worm-and-wheel final drive (for heavier vehicles). The latter was an elegant arrangement that combined a characteristically large gear ratio reduction with a right-angle drive, all in a package light enough to be fitted in a live rear axle. For overtype steam wagons there was no practical alternative to chain final drive but for most other heavy vehicles live axles had become practically universal by the late 1920s. America, oddly, was one of the last refuges of chain drive on production heavy lorries.

At the front end, it quickly became apparent that there was little scope for inventive axle designs. There have been attempts to popularise various forms of independent suspension, and thus break away from the time-honoured beam axle, but the few successes have been in the world of buses, especially luxury coaches. For lorries, the beam continues to reign supreme, and even the earlier efforts to avoid using the heavy stamping plant required to make the now almost-universal H-section axles by using round or square forged sections, or even built-up and riveted assemblies, came to nought.

The same is true of springing, where there have been many attempts to supersede plain, semi-elliptic multi-leaf springs, mounted in line with the chassis. Simplicity is not a quality to be lightly disregarded, but the sort of treatment endured by the suspension of a lorry gives rise to rapid wear and unpredictable breakages. Modern materials

Transmission complexities do not end with the gearbox: the drive has still to be turned through 90deg, and passed to the wheels. When tandem drive is employed the difficulties are not merely doubled, for in addition to the differential gears necessary in each axle, a third set is required to balance the drive between axles. This Leyland assembly also has reduction gears in each hub.

There is a great temptation, in a multi-axled machine, to lift wheels off the ground whenever possible in order to reduce tyre wear and tractive resistance. Fiat tried it with an eight-wheeler *(above)*, but drivers must have detected interesting changes in trailer behaviour, depending on whether the rearmost lorry wheels were up or down.

Saurer, for many years the major seminal influence in commercial vehicle development, has contrived to stay in the forefront of design despite being a small manufacturer in a small country. The four-wheeler *(left)* shows well the European predeliction for heavily built, good quality machines of therefore limited carrying capacity, which achieve economic versatility by hauling large drawbar trailers.

It is in the relatively uncomplicated field of semi-trailer engineering that most progress has been made in replacing conventional heavy and wear-prone multileaf springs. With no shackles or pins to lubricate, and the attractive characteristic of rubber in stiffening as the load on it is increased, a suspension of this kind can be light in weight and require hardly any maintenance.

Volvo has kept to steel leaves for its latest F10–12 range of tractors, but each leaf tapers from its centre in both directions. By anchoring the assembly at the front end, and mounting the trailing end in a slipper guide, the spring is effectively shortened and stiffened as the load on it increases.

and technology have made it possible to obtain sufficient flexibility in some applications without the need for separate leaves, two or three modern chassis thereby gaining the distinctive profiles of short, one-piece, bow-like springs.

An improvement pioneered by railway engineers was to incorporate some solid rubber components into the system: rubber bushes for spring shackles could be helpful in absorbing the kind of shock loading that cracks leaves.

The next step was to replace altogether the metallic elements in vehicle suspension – and this, too, was pioneered by railwaymen, when India rubber first became available in Europe. In more recent times a handful of rubber companies have produced resilient 'sandwiches' of rubber and steel which are flexible enough to absorb road shocks while still allowing full vertical articulation for multi-wheel bogies – all, it is claimed, while being maintenance-free. These solid rubber suspensions are finding favour with some semi-trailer makers and users, and one or two vehicle manufacturers are also prepared to fit them, usually to the rear axles of rigid six-wheelers operating on rough ground. Air suspension of the kind now common on buses and coaches throughout the world has yet to make much of a mark among lorry users, although its ability to respond in a satisfactory way to both full load and empty running (something difficult to achieve with most leaf-spring suspensions) has won a small but growing niche among the operators of tanker semi-trailers.

The biggest single advance in the steady development of heavy vehicles, however, was the shift from solid rubber to pneumatic tyres. From the very earliest experiments during the first decades of the nineteenth century, wheels and tyres had consistently proved the weakest and most troublesome part of every vehicle, large or small. The lesson was painfully relearned by the pioneers of the twentieth century. One thing was very clear: the age-old methods used by wheelwrights for horse-drawn vehicles simply could not cope with the wracking strains imposed by mechanical traction. The timber wheels were masterpieces of the woodworkers' art, but every one of the many beautifully-wrought joints was also a source of weakness.

Matters were made worse by the lack of suitable material for tyres. Wrought iron or steel in continuous hoops lasted for years at the walking pace of horses, but rapidly failed under the sustained pounding of much heavier vehicles. Rubber technology was soon able to provide solid rubber tyres acceptably durable for all but the weightiest lorries, but a largely unnecessary and industry-caused problem was an almost total lack of standardisation of wheel and tyre dimensions. There were differences of opinion over the comparative merits of large diameter versus small diameter wheels and other matters, but the tyre-making industry was heavily fragmented into separate warring factions, and there were obvious financial benefits in persuading makers and buyers to adopt tyres made to unique dimensions and obtainable from only one source. Common sense, and standardisation, began to prevail by 1914, when lesser battles of many kinds became submerged in the greater one, but it was not until the United States began to address itself to the business of mass-producing motor vehicles for war in 1917 that any determined efforts were made to reduce unnecessary variety: a measure of the problem was that it took a full year to secure agreement to condense 287 distinct tyre sizes into 32. By then pneumatic tyres were beginning to

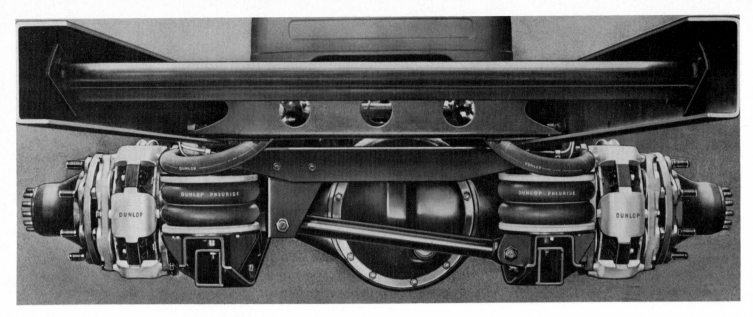

Dunlop sought, with this installation, to beguile manufacturers and users into adopting both air suspension and disc brakes on lorries. That was in the late-1950s, and neither proposal has made much advance.

appear and the makers had learnt their lesson – the old independence in the matter of sizing was not repeated.

Difficulties with wheels virtually disappeared when light and strong cast steel wheels became generally available. Solid rubber tyres moulded to thin backing rings and pressed on to cast steel wheels held sway for many years and gave standards of riding quality and operating economy that would surprise many present-day operators. Those spindly, comic-looking wheels of the 1920s were remarkably serviceable; only the general rise in vehicle speeds caused their rapid eclipse by the pneumatic tyre. Speed means heat, anathema to thick rubber, and solids could never provide the resilience needed to absorb the shocks to unsprung components – wheels, brakes and axles – resulting from such fast running.

Inflatable tyres for commercial vehicles, a development pioneered in France before the First World War but which owed much to American enterprise, began modestly on bicycles, was adopted for passenger cars and moved rapidly up the weight range: by 1918, 5 tonners mounted on pneumatics were regularly running at 50 km/h over long distances – if only in a series of experiments. Even so, in 1920 vehicles with a capacity of more than about 2 tonnes mounted on pneumatic tyres would have excited comment anywhere in the world. By 1930, no manufacturer was producing any quantity of conventional road vehicles – even the largest – on solids. Several factors caused this spectacular advance, among them the rapidly increasing numbers of vehicles coming into service (justifying development both of tyre and wheel equipment) and improvements in road construction. Good smooth roads, designed specifically for this new motor age, encouraged the growth of fast traffic. While the commercial vehicle of 1920 strongly resembled its parents of 1910 or even 1905, its offspring of 1930 were quite different, and conformed to a basic pattern that was to hold sway until the 1960s, when a new wave of road building swept road transport into its present form.

A factor often overlooked in surveying the development of mechanical traction on common roads is the humble but very necessary matter of braking. All too often, the realisation that the maximum speed of a vehicle is directly related to its ability to stop, has come as something of a surprise, sometimes even to designers. In the earliest days, the lack of suitable friction materials made it very difficult indeed to produce braking systems capable of performing reliably and consistently. Even after durable asbestos compounds became generally available, daunting problems remained: virtually every national authority insisted, on safety grounds, that each vehicle must have two quite separate braking systems; coupled with the practical difficulties of arranging reliable brakes on the front (steering) wheels, this made the whole business of stopping heavy vehicles one of the most intractable for designers.

Drum brakes with internally expanding shoes have to all intents and purposes been universal for many years, and the very few attempts to apply passenger car and aeroplane expertise in disc braking have not been commercially or even technically very successful. The object of any braking installation is to dissipate energy in the form of heat: sustained and considerable quantities of heat, produced during the slowing of a heavy commercial vehicle, are more than the materials currently available for discs can manage. The makers of drum brakes, on the other hand, have so far contrived to keep up with the demands made on them. Overall dimensions of the working components have slowly increased along with the general increase in vehicle and wheel sizes, but much of the credit really belongs to the laboratory technologists who have achieved steady improvements in the iron-based alloys used for drums, and in the materials used for linings.

The weight and speed of modern commercial vehicles are so great that it is quite impossible for human muscles to do anything very useful when it comes to stopping them. Instead, the medium used in virtually all modern heavy power braking systems is compressed air, and the driver has to exert no more effort than that required to open a control valve. Air has another great advantage in that it is very easy to pipe to wherever it is required. There is thus no difficulty at all in arranging a source of braking power to any and all the wheels in even the most complicated of articulated or drawbar road trains. Moreover, the flow of air is practically uniform in pressure and speed along each of its lines, so that in a properly maintained system all the wheels are equally retarded.

This latter characteristic is shared by hydraulic systems, of course, and these have achieved almost complete domination in passenger cars and light vans. Unfortunately, a hydraulic system does no more than transmit power, usually the effort exerted by the driver's foot. Pumps and servos could certainly be used more often to assist matters but, where large lorries are concerned, there would still be the problem of making and breaking joints in the hydraulic hoses connecting the brake circuits of tractors and trailers – a simple enough matter with air. In fact, compressed air meets the requirements of commercial vehicle users so well that it is not likely to be supplanted.

Vehicles are, of course, only half of any transport system, and the influence of contemporary road conditions on vehicle design cannot be overlooked. In 1900 those countries which had any proper roads were in the throes of awakening from the long railway-induced trance. Fuel of any kind was hard to find and roadside repair facilities were limited to such assistance as could be offered by an occasional farrier or wainwright. Indeed, so ill-equipped were nineteenth-century roads for the traffic about to pour on to them that most lacked even signposts; country carriers had no need of such things. Matters did change rapidly but meanwhile the best roads were paved with broken stone, rolled in by passing carts and steeply cambered to shed rain; the not-so-good were ill-drained rutted tracks. In many parts of the world, including America and most of the European colonies, paving of any kind between towns (and even in them) was largely unknown. One unfortunate result of this state of affairs was that vehicles had to be more heavily constructed than would otherwise have been the case – at a time when inferior materials meant that they were already very heavy in relation to payload. This additional weight inevitably had the effect of damaging poor roads yet further.

Unpaved roads were not the only kind unsuited to the motor era: some cities, seeking respite from the din of horses' hooves and iron-tyred carts, adopted wood paving. Square blocks of pine or similar timber were set in pitch on a level concrete base with the grain end-on; these were certainly durable and quiet – wood paving was sometimes used just outside churches and hospitals – but they were capable of striking terror into the hearts of any motor driver mounted on solid tyres on a damp and 'greasy' day. Squared stones, often granite, set in pitch on a sand base also lacked nothing in durability. Unfortunately, when the top surface was truly flat they offered little grip to either horse or motor; when the tops were domed or rounded, the resulting vibration to a heavy lorry was such as to make it prudent to offer a spanner to the chassis nuts and bolts afterwards. Just how bad stone paving can be is exemplified by the pavé of Belgium, which even now is a byword among connoisseurs of rough roads; no vehicle test track is considered complete without a stretch of simulated pavé, which is usually reckoned to accelerate wear two or three times.

The great drawback to unbound stones or gravel as a road paving material was dust. Iron tyres and slow speeds had the effect of gradually grinding each individual piece of stone to approximately uniform size, and the dust that resulted washed down into the joints and acted almost as a cement. Unfortunately, rubber tyres and high speeds were another matter, for they combined to produce a powerful suction effect that tended to lift stones clean out of the road; the dust which once had been beneficial was also sucked up and in dry weather it hung in dense choking clouds. Since it was also rich in pulverised animal droppings, this road dust was a potential health hazard as well as a major nuisance. At first, passenger cars were the main culprits, for they were both fast and had pneumatic tyres, but commercial vehicles soon began to speed up, and their size created large areas of air swirl which were very effective at raising the hated dust. All manner of palliatives were tried, from the ineffectual – like frequent spraying with water – to the messy – including coats of crude oil. Those territories with access to it quickly adopted coal tar, a cheap material readily obtainable from coal gas-making plants, and which had the useful property of being practically solid in most temperate climates while readily liquifying to a consistency suitable for spraying when heated. Tar used on its own developed a lethally slippery surface in wet weather but that hazard could easily be overcome by dressing the tar while it was still hot with pea-sized gravel.

Of course, the real solution came, as solutions so often do, when public outcry and economic need combined. The joint keys were asphalt, that curious derivative of natural or artificial mineral oil, and mass-concrete. Price differences sometimes favour one or the other, but both are particularly useful in that they are initially plastic materials capable of being readily formed on site. Until quite recent times, much laborious work went into preparing a sub-structure – levelling and consolidating the ground – and laying paving material; but civil engineering equipment has also advanced and a superb multi-lane highway can now be built in a few months, with a range of great machines capable of cutting valleys through hills and bridging defiles. Perhaps the most wonderful machines of all are the giant pavers, able to lay a continuous slab of road 6m wide and maybe 35cm thick, and capable of doing so across a continent if need be, just so long as their hoppers are kept full. That, of course, is a task that can only be performed by convoys of heavy lorries, which brings the story full circle.

Most of the early roads, poor as they were, were available free of charge to whoever wished to use them. Now, the costs of road construction are so high that many nations find it necessary to levy tolls on the users of their roads, bridges and tunnels. These fees are usually intended just to meet the capital cost of the facility but somehow they never quite achieve the goal, and road charging (in addition to all the other forms of taxation levied on commercial transport) is likely to endure for a very long time.

LIMITED PROGRESS 1900-1930

Very few buses, and even fewer lorries have been built without a chassis frame, despite the fact that almost all passenger car designers gave up separate chassis in favour of integral construction for their mass-produced vehicles 30 or 40 years ago. The reason is simple: cars are intended to be sold in great quantities and with little more than cosmetic differences between individual units; commercial vehicles, on the other hand, are produced in much smaller numbers and manufacturers can be sure that one basic model will enter service in many different guises. Relatively low output implies a considerable degree of handwork – there is not much economic scope for the sort of computerised robot machinery that can very nearly assemble a passenger car without human assistance – while the multi-purpose rôle indicates a need to combine a limited variety of major components in the maximum number of combinations. Both conditions are most easily met if mechanical units are mounted in some sort of frame. That frame is the chassis.

Chassis frames may broadly be divided into two main classes: those of pressed sheet steel, which began to find general acceptance about 1910 and which have reigned almost unchallenged since the late 1920s; and the various makeshift forms of construction that preceded pressed steel. Irrespective of the detailed construction, nearly all heavy vehicle chassis frames bear at least some resemblance to a ladder with widely spaced rungs. Side members provide the main strength of the assembly while the cross members give the structure its form and are shaped to make it easier to mount the main components.

As in so many matters relating to motor vehicles, chassis design appears straightforward and simple but turns out to be nothing of the sort. The biggest single difficulty is that the loads imposed along a chassis are all unequal, and some constantly change. The engine, for example, is almost invariably over or very near the front wheels and presents a heavy constant weight at one end; this encourages the other, often lightly loaded, end to swing up and down rather like a pendulum.

The payload on the other hand is imposed over the rear parts of the frame, and its effect depends on the type of cargo and the way it is loaded. Long lengths of timber or steel pipes will spread the burden effectively; a cargo of heavy canned food, to be delivered to several shops, will impose quite different loads after each part-offloading. Matters can be hindered or helped by the bodywork fitted: a tanker is inherently stiff and can easily put an intolerable strain on a flexible chassis, but a flat tray body offers little resistance to any weaving by the chassis frame.

Then there are stresses caused by running over even quite smooth-surfaced roads, and the twisting movements that result whenever one wheel happens to be standing a little higher or lower than its fellows. Add to these the forces caused by braking or negotiating corners, and it is not surprising that vehicle makers were and occasionally still are plagued by cracked and broken chassis.

Several early makers, searching for something that could be adapted to their own needs, looked at rolled steel structural sections, usually of channel or H-section. The advantages were real: cheapness and ready availability in almost any lengths, with flat surfaces that made it easy to joint them and to add the multitude of plates and brackets necessary to mount all the other vehicle components. The disadvantages were real too: because the members were uniform in cross-section throughout

Conventional ideas on what lorries should look like can sometimes be confounded by the need to meet special requirements. Usually materials like steel reinforcing bars and structural sections can be carried easily enough on ordinary flat semi-trailers, but occasionally a rigid self-propelled vehicle is required – and length is at a premium. The chassis under this sample was by Henschel.

their length, local reinforcing was often necessary to meet the uneven loadings, and these additions added to the inevitable weight penalty that came from using material intended for a very different purpose. Even so, rolled steel channel served well enough to launch such famous companies as Daimler in Germany, who used it on their earliest buses and lorries up to 4·5 tonnes gross weight; both Maudslay and Clarkson in England; and most of the steam wagon builders. The great drawback of rolled steel channel as a ready-made material for commercial vehicle chassis is the additional bracing that is often required: some used queen post trussing reminiscent of that still common on railway carriages, while Maudslay riveted on extra, deep steel plates, one inside each member. Such precautions were deemed unnecessary by Guy, one of the last volume users of rolled channel, who adopted it for a range of 1·25–1·5 tonne chassis during the 1920s.

A surprising choice of material by both AEC (a company founded as an offshoot of the main London bus company) and the British Daimler concern, was wood. Faced with the problem of producing maximum capacity vehicles with a stringent gross weight limit, these two makers decided to use planks of ash for the side members and main cross members of their chassis. The timber was faced on both sides with a thin steel plate, and the whole riveted together. A great many vehicles for passenger and goods carrying were made in this unlikely manner and gave great satisfaction, although chassis built by these companies to the same general design but expressly for freight carrying used conventional pressed steel chassis. Even so, hundreds of London buses were made with chassis largely of wood as late as 1921.

Despite these distractions it was clear from a very early date that pressed steel offered so many advantages that its universal use would eventually

become inevitable. Given big enough press tools, and a sufficiently large demand, sheet steel may be formed into an almost infinite variety of shapes. Chassis side members can be profiled to match exactly the demands placed on them – slimly-lined webs over the front axle where loads are at a minimum; deep under the back wall of the cab, at the point where so many chassis have broken; tapered away at the tail. The top and bottom flanges, too, can be widened locally to provide rigid fixings for the chassis cross members – which can be pressed and pierced to provide perfect mount-

Traditionally, high quality chassis were assembled with hand-fitted bolts and nuts, and great durability resulted. Nowadays not only is there a greater appreciation of the fact that there is little point in any part of a vehicle outlasting the economic life of the whole, but modern riveting can match the performance of more expensive practices.

ings for major items, such as the gearbox, with maximum strength and minimum weight. The only drawback is the enormous expense of retooling for a brand new shape, but it was not long before the specalist makers devised ways of assembling specially-shaped die tools from existing stocks of separate part-tools, whereupon quite short production runs became feasible. For special applications it is not difficult to add extra reinforcement in the form of either simple flat plates or 'sleeves' – pressed sections secured inside the chassis channels. By the 1920s, pressed steel chassis were almost universal, and were outwardly very similar (although smaller) to those still in use. There have

been changes in detail, notably in the steadily improving alloy steels that have become available over the years and have done much to reduce weight, and in methods of assembly. Welding has never been favoured for these fabrications, for there are well-founded suspicions about the resistance to stress fatigue in such structures, and for a long time riveting was regarded as suitable only for cheaper products; hand-fitted bolts, needing to be lightly hammered into their holes, were considered essential for good quality chassis until quite recent times, although modern patent cold-setting rivets are now supplanting the time-consuming bolts.

One other interesting chassis form deserves mention for its persistence – the centre spine. The Czech Tatra company began using it more than half a century ago and uses it still; in the form adapted by that concern the spine is a large diameter tube in which are housed the propeller shaft and differential unit. The engine is supported in a cradle at the front and a simple form of independent suspension with swinging arms is used all round. Tatra has made every kind of commercial vehicle in this way, from small and medium-sized four and six-wheeled lorries and buses during the 1920s to giant eight-wheel-drive gun tractors in more recent times.

Engine design settled down quickly: by about 1904 the exterior form had assumed a shape that was to be familiar for the next 25 years, although changes were rapid after about 1930, the year that emphasised so many changes of direction in commercial vehicle design.

The classic engine was a four cylinder petrol unit, often with the cylinders in pairs, probably in cast iron and bolted to a roomy crankcase, also cast, but often in an aluminium-based light alloy. Pistons were cast iron, beautifully moulded and machined for lightness, while the forged connecting rods had lead-tin alloy crankhead bearings cast in – there were no separate linings then. The shortcomings of bearing design, contemporary metallurgy and lubrication techniques were clearly evidenced by the large access hand-holes that featured in the sidewalls of a great many crankcases. Replacing bear-

ings of all kinds was not considered an untoward roadside repair until the last lorries of the 1920s were off the road. Something that did change more quickly was the total dependence on the 'feast-or-famine' engine oil supply inevitable with unassisted splash lubrication. Motor vehicles produced enough smoke and smell without the additional emanations that resulted when more oil than necessary was thrown about the cylinder walls. Pressure lubrication tended to reduce that nuisance and helped make bearing life more predictable.

The general lack of durability had further mute testimony at the top end of the engine, for nearly all cylinder heads (most of them non-detachable, because of the difficulty in making satisfactory head-to-cylinder-block joints) were adorned with large screwed-in caps, usually of brass, which gave ready access to the poppet valves. But in those early days, valves were commonly made with cast iron heads and screwed-in mild steel stems, case hardened.

Water was rarely forsaken as the cooling medium in those old engines, and as soon as the old-style steam condenser radiator was supplanted by the multi-tubular kind that is still so familiar, water served very well indeed. Much reliance was placed on the thermo-syphon principle for adequate circulation, so the hottest water was allowed to rise naturally to the top of the water jackets surrounding the cylinders, thence to the radiator where it cooled and sank. Increasingly, pumps were incorporated to help improve circulation and reduce size, and a large fan, belt-driven from the

front of the crankshaft, aided matters by drawing air through the radiator. Despite all this, a large and constantly replenished water can was an essential at every stopping place that sought to attract lorry drivers.

A side effect of this satisfactory if simple system of cooling was that radiators, positioned to derive maximum benefit from any available breeze, were inevitably conspicuous. The radiator, indeed, was for many years the most prominent feature at the front end of almost every motor vehicle, and manufacturers took good care to adopt designs visually

unlike those of anyone else. In the days before
wholesale standardisation of cab and body styling,
the radiator was usually the main recognition feature, too. The products of those few factories that
did not fit front radiators were automatically distinctive: in France, Renault and Latil put their radiators
behind the engines and produced unmistakable
front hoods; the British-built Tilling-Stevens
company briefly produced a passable imitation of
the Renault look for its very first production
petrol-electrics; Austin tried something akin to
the Latil-look for its short-lived twin-shaft lorries;
International Harvester introduced a rear-
radiatored lorry during the last year of the First
World War. Only the French persevered to overcome the cooling problems inherent with this
scheme and their reward may have been more
uniform running temperatures and less dirt in the
radiator matrices.

Many and varied have been the designs tried by
inventors seeking to overcome the time-honoured
definition of a carburettor as 'a device designed to
supply the wrong quantities of petrol to an engine at
all speeds'; since the battle has still to be totally
won, it follows that carburation during the first three
decades of the century left something to be
desired. General opinion soon settled in favour of a
large, single carburettor, capable of supplying all
the cylinders without the efficiency of the twin and
triple installations common in passenger cars, but
with a much greater likelihood of remaining
properly adjusted. The fact that most had a great
deal of easily polished brass and copper about
them added considerably to the underbonnet
appearance of vehicles whose drivers frequently
took great pride in their charges.

In the days before increased road speeds and
improved lamp-making made electric lighting both

necessary and possible, most owners avoided the
need for expensive and unreliable batteries by
using magneto ignition. Magnetoes are a species of
generator, directly driven by the engine, and capable of producing a large and powerful spark, even
at the low speeds at which a large engine can be
hand-cranked for starting. The use of a battery with
a dynamo to keep it charged opened the way for
coil ignition of the kind familiar to most modern
motorists – magnetoes never quite shook off a
reputation for being mysterious and unpredictable
devices. Soon after that diesel engines, which have
no need for any external means of igniting their
fuel, began to dominate the scene.

The petrol engine must keep running during all
but the longest stops, so that some means had to
be found to disconnect at will the engine from its
drive train. Many and varied have been the
attempts to replace the time-honoured friction
clutch with something less brutal in its action.
Electro-magnetic clutches, in which a variable electric current provided the slippage necessary for an
engine to 'pick up' its load from rest, beguiled
designers from the earliest days but – despite
determined attempts – they never managed to
equal the demands made on them. Hydraulic
devices, too, seemed to offer great possibilities –
indeed, fluid drive ultimately became an essential
component in most automatic and semi-automatic
transmissions. For a long time, however, the extra
complication of pumps and piping, and the great
difficulty in getting fluid-tight joints and seals, militated against the system. Nowadays, incidentally,
hydraulic power systems invariably use mineral oil
as the fluid but it was not always so: at least one
hopeful inventor used water, and while he may
have overcome some sealing problems, the prospect of endless corrosion and low temperature

difficulties should have been enough to warn off anyone possessed of imagination.

So the field was dominated by friction clutches, for which vehicle engineers had to be content with distinctly unpromising materials until Herbert Frood perfected his woven and compressed asbestos fabric linings, which offered unprecedentedly high coefficients of friction. Leather, that panacea for so many technical problems in early automobilism, inevitably loomed large; it served well enough as the essential component in the contemporary cone clutches, but it was totally unsuitable for the few plate clutches of the day, and manufacturers of these had therefore to persevere with metal facings. The cone clutch became virtually standard, with a truncated female cone – really a recess with a bevelled perimeter – machined in to the engine flywheel. Mounted concentrically with it, and in front of a separate gearbox, was the male half of the clutch, around whose rim was riveted a band of leather. A very heavy spring kept the two members firmly together, so transmitting the drive. Eventually asbestos linings replaced the leather, until the late 1920s when technology made plate clutches both more certain in their action and vastly more durable. It was a development which marked another step away from the old self-sufficiency of most motor manufacturers – almost anyone could make a cone clutch, but the greater complication of the newer units created a further opening for specialist suppliers.

There were two other lines of thought worth mentioning because of their long-term implications. Ford, in its early days a remarkably innovative concern, used an epicyclic gearbox for its popular Model-T cars and trucks; it was a lead followed by few other makers until W. G. Wilson perfected a combination of self-contained fluid clutch and epicyclic gearbox which became universally known as the preselector type, and as such became not only a standard fitting on urban buses, but also the parent of whole families of semi- and fully automatic transmissions.

Also interesting were the multi-plate clutches, in which a pack of metallic plates gradually separating or closing gave a smooth drive take-up. In the early 1900s Fiat used a 60-steel-plate unit (at just the moment when de Dion was extolling the virtues of a single plate, albeit of bronze) and the English scientist Prof. Hele-Shaw was promoting his version of the multi-plate clutch, with its alternate thin steel and bronze discs, each with a circumferential corrugation. Like so many technical leads in commercial vehicle design, these were aimed at improving the lot of bus passengers, and any that found their way into goods vehicles did so almost by accident. Things are not much better today, but the multi-plate pack is almost universal in the drivelines and braking of heavy earthmoving and civil engineering plant.

An unfortunate characteristic of the internal combustion engine is its inability to do anything very useful unless it is running at a high and fairly constant speed. It is therefore imperative that some means be adopted to match engine speed to road speed, and after some early irrelevancies like belt drive with fast-and-loose pulleys, and various friction devices, the only real contenders were the

Panhard-style gearbox, with its wheels sliding sideways into mesh (it was brusque and brutal, but it undoubtedly worked), and the constant mesh gearbox. In the latter, as the name implies, the gearwheels are saved the frightful grinding suffered by their sliding counterparts: instead, positive-drive dog clutches inside the box engage and disengage at the driver's will. An apparently attractive variation on this theme was the Linley, whose powerful springs held the dog clutch of a chosen ratio out of mesh until either the throttle lifted or the clutch dipped. Its effect was to give the driver many of the advantages of a preselector, and the resultant performance was a strong selling point for Commer Cars, whose chief engineer was for many years Mr Linley.

The greatest and most intractable fault of all the early gearboxes was noise, caused by an imperfectly understood theory of geartooth form, and by inadequate machining and heat treatment techniques. AEC overcame the problem in a most

Early gearboxes – this is a British Daimler – had the great attribute of being simple, with straight-toothed gears engaged and disengaged by sliding sideways. Unfortunately it took great sleight of hand to change gear cleanly, and in any case there was always a great deal of noise from the gearwheels.

Compelled by the licensing authorities to find quieter transmissions for its London buses, AEC produced a silent chain version. Teeth formed inside the chains engaged with gearwheels, and ratios were changed by sliding small internal clutches into and out of engagement.

Roller chains worked well enough in the final drives of heavy vehicles when speeds were low, but while simplicity is often a virtue it can sometimes verge upon the crude. Some users were willing to accept, on medium weight lorries, the higher cost of inverted tooth chains: in recompense they got quieter, faster running and less snatching in the transmission.

ingenious design that served the company and its customers loyally for years. It was, essentially, a constant mesh layout, but instead of the gearwheel teeth meshing directly they were connected by short chains, each formed of flat plate links shaped to form gear teeth across the inner sides of the chains. Popular opinion among competitors was that such inverted tooth chains, running at short centres and with no means of adjustment, would not prove durable; in practice they lasted very well indeed, and many of these AEC boxes outlived their first chassis and were salvaged for a new lease of life in a second. The shortlived Scottish-built Lothian chassis and others of the same period tried similar boxes; one real disadvantage was the higher cost of manufacture.

If noise was a major shortcoming of early gear technology, size and weight were hardly less important. Heavy gearboxes in particular were something of a drawback in those underpowered and low capacity early chassis, but at least the weight could be accommodated, if only by losing some payload capacity. Unfortunately, this pragmatic approach was and is quite impracticable for load-carrying axles, which are also expected to transmit drive to the road. While turning the drive through a right-angle (nearly every goods-carrying chassis so far has had its engine crankshaft aligned along the chassis), the final drive unit must also include provision for allowing either wheel to turn considerably faster than its mate, while fairly sharing the engine power between them. In addition, the axle must be able to absorb and transmit the full power of the engine, multiplied by the gearbox and differential ratios. All these considerations create great weight – in a unit where weight is a big disadvantage, for while the shock loadings caused to and by much of a vehicle structure are cushioned by its springs, the only springing enjoyed by most forms of axle are the tyres.

In the early days, such a concept was clearly out of the question, and for a few years after the turn of the century even makers of the more powerful passenger cars had to rely on side chains for a light, strong and reliable final drive; commercial vehicle manufacturers continued to do so until well after the First World War. For lorries and buses

chains offered some attractive advantages: the differential unit could be incorporated in a counter-shaft unit as large and as heavy as it needed to be, for it was bolted firmly underneath the chassis frame, conveniently out of the way. The axle itself needed to be no more than a simple forged steel beam, for it was 'dead' – that is, fixed – and the road wheels revolved independently on its ends.

Experience soon showed that roller chains exposed to the harsh operating conditions of lorry final drives in the days of unsealed road surfaces were best kept as short as possible, although wear could be taken up by the simple expedient of moving the axle bodily backwards. Looking for quicker running and a little more general refinement, some makers adopted the saw-like inverted tooth chain, at least one brand of which used ingenious two-part link pins that were alleged to compensate for wear. The countershaft unit was sometimes incorporated in the gearbox, but most designers found it more expedient to keep the two assemblies separate, and to transmit drive from one to the other with a cardan shaft similar to the one which linked clutch and gearbox.

Another early difficulty was the lack of suitable universal joints, capable of absorbing the fluctuating alignments which are unavoidable in the drive line of any long vehicle. The problem was eased considerably on chain-drive chassis by mounting the engine, gearbox and countershaft more or less rigidly in line in one frame; on vehicles with 'live' axles, where the final length of propeller shaft was constantly moving up and down, the flexible joints were under considerable stress. In practice, leather discs served well enough until the mid-1920s, when modern Hardy Spicer variations of the eighteenth century Hooke's joint began their progress towards almost total domination of this small but vital element of vehicle anatomy.

In theory, the simplest form of live, or driving, axle needed no more than a pair of bevel gears; indeed, many manufacturers used bevels. Unfortunately the result was usually noisy, for the short-comings in gear design and manufacture were present here too, and the short length of each gear tooth made them liable to wear and breakage. In addition, contemporary road speeds were such that bevels could not produce sufficiently large ratio reductions, and another pair of gears often had to be incorporated somewhere in the axle, adding to weight and noise.

Happily, there was a solution to these difficulties that was at once straightforward and reliable, and two British companies – Dennis Brothers and Daimler – followed by the Swiss Berna concern, spent much effort in perfecting worm reduction gear for vehicle final drives. In its simplest form, this combination comprises a multi-start screw-threaded worm engaging with the teeth of a gear-wheel: at once it turns the drive line through 90 degrees, while the geometry provides a considerable speed reduction that usually obviates the need for other integral reduction gearing. Since the input (worm) and output (wheel) shafts cannot be on the same centreline, it is also possible to have either a low level propeller shaft or excellent ground clearance, depending on whether the worm is above or below the axle. Since the action of worm and wheel

The gear elements in live driving axles must be able to accept heavy and fluctuating loads, while providing large speed reductions. One approach was to use bevel gears for the initial stage, with a further reduction housed in the main assembly – like this c.1914 Pagefield axle *(left)*. A distinct improvement is the Scammell of half a century later *(centre)*, which has helical teeth for the bevel wheels and an epicyclic secondary reduction, an arrangement that gives a big step down in a reliable and compact form.

is essentially a sliding one, the whole is virtually noiseless, and it is light in weight into the bargain.

Worm drive was very widely adopted – indeed, it is far from dead now – until the great advances in gear design that came about with the explosive growth of motoring between the wars gave the industry special bevel and helical gears capable of withstanding the enormous loadings inherent in commercial vehicle operation.

Some early makers did try hard to resist the near-universal predeliction for side-chain final drives. Daimler began a minor trend in adopting what it called rack and pinion for its early commercial vehicles, although the arrangement was not the one usually pictured by engineers when they use that definition. The Daimler racks were internally-toothed ring gears, a little smaller in diameter than the rims of the rear wheels – which revolved on a light dead axle – and bolted inside them. The pinions were mounted one at each end of a counter-shaft, and permanently engaged the racks. Thus, in one move, Daimler obtained a sizeable speed reduction at the road wheels, which meant that the rest of the drive line could turn more quickly and therefore use smaller, lighter, components.

The drawbacks were rapid wear and then tremendous noise. Protecting the final drive from road grit and mud proved too difficult for Daimler and the company sometimes suffered the mortification of having its products radically altered by users after a year or two of running experience. While Daimler turned to other solutions, Berna in Switzerland adopted what amounted to a fully enclosed version of the idea, while Daimler compatriot MAN took the idea of separate axle and drive-shafts, but used ordinary gears to obtain a more modest speed reduction. That was during the mid-1920s, and MAN uses such axles still.

In Britain, Austin attempted to obtain the best of both chain and shaft worlds on a range of trucks introduced a couple of years before the First World War. The differential was mounted midway along a beautifully detailed and constructed pressed-steel chassis; two propeller shafts, diagonally placed, took the drive to small bevel boxes just inside the

Since it combined light weight, a big speed reduction, and was virtually noiseless, the worm drive axle could be sure of a welcome among early vehicle builders and users. Unfortunately it was also expensive, and a little neglect would soon ruin it.

Several makers in the earliest years separated the load-carrying and propelling functions of back axles by mounting the wheel assemblies on the ends of beam axles and transmitting the drive through secondary shafts that carried none of the vehicle weight. Unlike the rest, MAN persevered with the idea and still does: this chassis *(bottom)* is a diesel powered 2·5 tonner of 1935 and shows how the propeller shaft passed through the axle proper; the close-up *(below)* illustrates how MAN used the arrangement to obtain a further speed reduction within the wheel hubs.

rear wheels, which revolved on a dead axle. At much the same time that Austin contemplated abandoning its twin propeller shafts, the American Atlas company took them up, though not for long. An equally unconventional and complicated attempt to avoid chains was the celebrated de Dion axle, which in one application or another has remained in favour for eight decades. It was yet another design that sought to separate the two functions of a drive axle, and it did so by mounting the differential unit in the chassis above a dead axle and transmitting the drive to the wheel centres with short half shafts. This demands the provision of four extra universal joints, one at each end of each shaft, in order that the dead axle can move up and down on its springs, but unsprung weight is kept to a minimum despite this apparent drawback and the arrangement has worked well on all kinds of vehicles, from small passenger cars to heavy lorries.

Passenger cars and light van makers without doubt face many of the problems of braking which also confront their commercial vehicle contemporaries, but at least the forces they have to contend with are less. Hydraulic systems are almost universally used as the means of expanding brake shoes in the drums of light vehicles. Before

hydraulics (which means roughly 1930) some factories relied on wire cables, with pulley wheels wherever a change of direction was necessary. But cables stretch and pulley bearings wear and most makers therefore relied on steel rods for the tension links. So too did heavy vehicle manufacturers, although some found that problems caused by the much longer lengths required could be nicely overcome by using steel ribands in place of rods.

From an early period means were sought to lessen the physical effort required to slow and stop heavy vehicles, and a common provision for many years was a vacuum servo – a piston and cylinder assembly built into the brake rigging and deriving its vacuum from the engine air intake; a little vacuum could be made to do a lot of work. A full mechanical linkage was kept for emergencies and for when the engine was not running, but with servo assistance drivers could safely handle all but the heaviest vehicles. A minor complication came with the diesel engine, for diesels take their air in a steady flow and do not produce a usable vacuum. The answer was to add a small exhauster to the engine-driven accessories. Steam powered vehicles had no difficulty at all in producing all the vacuum they might require for braking or any other purpose (including filling their own water tanks) with the aid of an injector. One or two makers, naturally enough, also tried steam powered brakes.

All these mechanically linked systems met considerable difficulty at the end of the 1920s when the time came to consider seriously the application of brakes to the front wheels. The problems stemmed from the fact that although steering wheels are required to swing from side to side, any braking effort must be absolutely uniform whatever the position of the wheels and must also be in balance with the rear wheels. Designers of small vehicles had little choice but to persevere with arrangements of cranks and levers, placing the vital change-of-direction pivots precisely over or under the steering kingpins. Commercial vehicle steering components were sometimes large enough to drill the pivot holes along the kingpins, which overcame one problem at the expense of servicing convenience.

After about 1930, when braking layouts were standardised and service brakes were applied by a foot pedal to all wheels, the hand-lever-operated brake was essentially for parking purposes, or as a means of impeding progress in times of emergency. Invariably, a separate linkage was used, usually to expand the rear brake shoes only, although it sometimes applied a brake mounted on the propeller shaft. Before four-wheel braking, however, there was considerable diversity, and the hand lever played a much more prominent role; quite often it was actually the service brake.

The understandable desire to have two independent braking systems on every vehicle, even in the early days, led to some interesting variety. Some manufacturers used wider brake drums than usual and installed two pairs of expanding shoes, mounted side by side. Others used drums with one pair of expanding shoes inside each rim and a contracting pair on the outside. This certainly tended to equalise stresses, but it worsened the ever-present problem of heat. Many designers cast calculating eyes on the propeller shaft and fitted brakes, usually of the contracting variety, to it. The attractions were real: since the shaft always revolves at a much higher speed than the wheels, a brake drum mounted on it can be very much smaller than its wheel-mounted counterpart. What is more, its effect is applied evenly, irrespective of the differential gear, to both wheels, something that could rarely be claimed for wheel brakes. Unfortunately the main drawback was equally real, and a distressingly large number of propeller shaft joints proved unequal to the violent strain thrown upon

them by vigorous applications of the brakes, whereupon, of course, all engine braking was also lost. Heat, the generation of which is in a sense one of the major objects of a braking system, was particularly troublesome in those early, small-diameter fast-turning transmission brakes and a few makers even incorporated water cooling.

Nearly every manufacturer using chain final drive also incorporated braking on the countershaft, for it offered a useful compromise between the high speed of the propeller shaft and the low speed of the road wheels while also keeping the brake assemblies out of the worst of the road dirt. The usual scheme involved a drum at each end of the shaft, to which were mounted the final chain pinions; some contained expanding shoes, most had contracting bands. The all-pervading problem for every maker, and in triple-distilled form for every driver, was the lack of any suitable material to provide friction in brakes. For the walking speeds attained by heavy horse-drawn vehicles the simplest and crudest devices sufficed: a long lever arranged to press a block of wood against one of the hind wheels served to slow progress in traffic, and the sole of an old boot helped protect the wood. For a very few years at the very beginning of the motor era, when heavy vehicles were no larger or faster than the wagons they sought to replace, and also had steel tyres, they too used tyre brakes. But not for long.

Timber linings lasted a few years longer for band brakes but cast iron shoes applied to cast iron drums had to serve for most, and a measure of the inadequacy of this arrangement was the oil can

Eloquent, if mute, testimony to the lack of faith by both manufacturers and users in the braking systems available during the first 20 years of motor road transport. The sprag brake was nothing more than a stout steel bar hung under the rear of the chassis so that it could be dropped at will to bite into the road and prevent run-back. Wise drivers lowered the sprag in good time: too late, and the vehicle would probably vault over it.

which drivers had to apply regularly and frequently to the contact surfaces. As soon as Herbert Frood (of Ferodo) introduced his asbestos-based friction materials, virtually every heavy vehicle manufacturer seized upon them and abandoned all others. At much the same time the music of the sprag also faded into history. The sprag was nothing more than a stout bar hinged firmly under the back end of a chassis and long enough to trail on the road surface. Drivers faced with a climb and lacking faith in their vehicle's braking simply unhooked the sprag and let it rattle along the road; at the first sign of a runback the sprag bit into the stones.

When Lankensperger of Munich patented his steering device for vehicles (the one more generally known by the name of his associate, Ackermann) he served posterity better than he knew, for his arrangement of stub-axle steering gear has never been bettered – or even seriously challenged. Lankensperger sought to improve the stability of horse-drawn vehicles during cornering: when all four wheels on a traditionally-built horse-drawn carriage are in line ahead the vehicle is stable; as the front axle is turned the base on which the wheels stand effectively narrows, until the stage is reached when the horse is at right-angles to its vehicle and the front axle is in line with it. A four-point base has become an unstable three-point one. This unsatisfactory state of affairs was entirely overcome by the Ackermann arrangements, for with careful design matters can be arranged so that each of the steering wheels pivots about the point on which it stands on the ground, and thus the four-square base on which the vehicle stands is unaffected. So good is the principle that with only one significant exception – most of the overtype steam wagons – it has ruled supreme during the mechanical era although, oddly enough, it was hardly tried on horse-drawn wagons and carriages.

Of the many intractable problems to cause the early commercial vehicle operators sleepless nights the worst, without much doubt, was the combined headache of wheels and tyres. It is hard to conceive of any possible combination of materials and principles that has not at some time or another been tried in the search for an adequate wheel. At the turn of the century two basic designs suitable for heavy vehicles were available: one was directly related to the all-steel wheels used on European-style steam traction engines, and comprised rolled rims and cast hubs connected by flat bar spokes; the alternative was not dissimilar in appearance, although made up from pressed and pierced steel discs. The great drawback was that these wheels offered no resilience at all. On agricultural engines, spending most of their lives in soft-surfaced fields, this rigidity was almost an advantage, although the vibration that assailed their crews whenever the engines ventured on to hard roads was excessive. Some surviving old engines have had solid rubber tyres mounted over the original treads and in this form are quite good enough for the low speeds they attain; in their youth, however, suitable rubber had yet to be evolved.

Wooden wheels, the only practical alternative to steel, were generally regarded as superior because of their greater resilience, even though much of their ability to absorb shocks resulted from the many joints flexing and, ultimately, loosening. Nearly all these heavy duty wooden wheels were of the so-called artillery type – the form was also widely used for guns – and they had a long and respectable history. One of the early nineteenth-century steam carriage makers, Walter Hancock, invented them. The principle of construction was that of an arch; based on a cast iron or steel hub, the spokes were cut at their inner ends so that they bedded solidly together. Then an iron or steel tyre, shrunken on to the wooden rim, served to lock it all together: sometimes, in an attempt to withstand the great strains caused by transmitting the drive, makers placed spokes tangentially. Looking at illustrations of those old wheels, the abiding impression they create is that wheelwrights found difficulty incorporating all the prime oak and ash that they wished; even so, their handiwork soon disintegrated under the combined assaults of cobbled roads and the snatch of driving chains.

So unsatisfactory were these earliest heavy wheels that by 1910 cast steel ruled for all new chassis. Upon the coming of pneumatic tyres 12 to 15 years later a distinct divergence of opinion appeared. Some makers, notably in Britain, adopted detachable pressed steel wheels for every size of vehicle; others preferred spoked cast steel wheels with detachable rims for their larger products.

The desperation felt by the first motor lorry men

Wood served well enough for passenger car wheels and also for those on light weight commercial vehicles. Regular and frequent attention was needed to prevent rapid deterioration.

On heavy lorries (far right) wood had limitations as a material for wheel construction. Once wheels had reached this degree of solidity no more timber could be added. The clips, incidentally, are for snow chains.

about tyres can still be sensed in even a cursory look at some of the strange devices with which inventors and makers sought to woo them. Spring wheels of one sort or another abounded, the hope being that the evident shock-absorbing advantages of rubber might be obtained with far more durability. Not a few designs were variations of a basic plan that involved many coil springs placed radially between hub and rim; one comprised a sealed chamber filled with small balls – the inventor claimed they would vibrate into the most suitable form to carry the load. None were of any lasting use: the combined effects of road dirt in the complicated internal workings of such wheels, and the stress of transmitting driving and braking effort was too much.

So designers were thrown back to finding a resilient tyre. Wood, in the form of blocks with the grain running radially, served after a style, and were probably a little better when a layer of rubber was interposed between the blocks and the wheel rim. One inventor tried blocks of elm impregnated with rubber; another compressed paper. Many makers tried solid rubber in blocks, which could not only be individually replaced when damaged, but which were also held to offer some protection against skidding and the universally dreaded side-slip. It is quite forgotten, now, that in the days of animal traction city streets were covered in a layer of mud and droppings, euphemistically called 'grease'. Combined with an underlying pavement of smooth granite or wood blocks, skidding was a constant and dangerous hazard, and motorists of all kinds were in a permanent agony of indecision over how best to combat the risk. Very narrow treads cut through the slime, but wore quickly; studded leather bands disintegrated more quickly still; rope became lumpy and out of round; little brushes on blades mounted in front of each wheel to sweep away the filth fell off. By 1920 motor vehicles were well on the way to solving the problem for themselves – simply by supplanting the horse. By 1930 pneumatic tyres with wide, scientifically designed treads had turned sideslipping into a forgotten thing, and skids became things that usually happened only on ice.

Much of the credit for this satisfactory rate of progress must go to Goodyear in America, although Michelin and Firestone were also doing valuable work: Michelin, indeed, had the temerity to put a 2·5 tonne truck on pneumatics before the First World War, even though conventional wisdom five or six years later still held that 2 tonnes was the sensible upper limit for pneumatics. By that time, however, user experience was beginning to accumulate, with casing lives of 40,000 km being reported. What was more, owners were beginning to notice much reduced wear and tear on those vehicles which had forsaken solid tyres, despite covering greater distances. The real turning point came when Goodyear, as soon as the war ended, began an intensive series of practical experiments, putting pneumatic tyres on vehicles ferrying supplies and finished goods to and from the factory. The most spectacular of these was a box-bodied four-wheel-drive Walter tractor, hauling a pair of 5 tonne capacity drawbar trailers: this combination was running 1300 km journeys (including mountain

Cast steel spoked wheels (above) had the virtue of being tough and light, while they could be made with existing materials and techniques. Extra bracing for heavier loads was easily incorporated.

Pressed steel (left), with the separate components welded together, have held sway in many parts of the world for the last half century. They are comparatively light, easily and cheaply made as mass-production items, and withstand ill-treatment.

Some manufacturers, notably in America, Germany, and Italy, prefer detachable rims, an arrangement which leaves the wheel proper on the vehicle. This preference has become reinforced over the years as the size and weight of tyres and wheels has increased.

passes) at averages of 40 km/h with nearly 60 km/h maximum speed. Air braking was fitted and – a rare accessory on delivery vehicles – the tractor had a winch which it used for recovering itself and its train when roads collapsed, and for hauling its trailers into and out of underground loading docks.

A fleet of more conventional vehicles – rigid six-

wheelers with double drive, braking on four wheels, and carrying capacities of 5 tonnes – soon began running. Troubles there certainly were, but the company had made up its mind to succeed and this team of mobile test-beds made success possible and not too elusive.

Almost simultaneously, incidentally, both Norway and Holland took prophetic steps by proposing laws that would favour pneumatic tyres and penalise solids.

Not that the old ways surrendered without a struggle. Off-road work (which in those days was generally taken to mean quarries and perhaps building sites paved with broken brick) was, the experts generally agreed, not a task for pneumatics. And while the new tyres might have a place in fast light work, heavy transport demanded something more robust. Tyre makers, facing the huge expense of the new technology, claimed to have found the solution to complaints of vibration and bad ride with a new idea: cushion, or semi-pneumatic tyres which looked like solids but which had a hollow unpressurised core. But it was all to no avail. The future was to ride on air, although for a year or two many users adopted the awkward-looking compromise of leaving solids at the rear while converting the front wheels to pneumatics.

Trailers of two kinds have dominated road transport from the earliest days to the present time. The natural and most obvious way of increasing the carrying capacity of any vehicle is to hitch to it another, capable of supporting a load on its own wheels and requiring only to be hauled along – in short, a drawbar trailer. With very little difficulty the capacity of the tractor vehicle is at once doubled, something particularly useful during the years when the unladen weight of a lorry often equalled or exceeded its payload capacity. There was no need

at all for such a trailer to be in the least complicated, and few were. Occasional efforts were made to improve the steering characteristics of drawbar trailers, for the cut-in of the rearmost trailer wheels when cornering (the radius followed by the wheels compared to the much larger circle described by the front wheels of the tractor vehicle) has always been a nuisance.

But when speeds of lorries running solo rarely exceeded (legally) 12–20 km/h, the speed they were permitted when hauling a trailer was often only half that, so that braking requirements were hardly onerous. It was usually sufficient to rely on drum or band brakes fitted to the trailer rear wheels and pulled on by a cable-operated ratchet lever or screw worked from the lorry cab by the driver's mate. In some places it became the custom for a brakesman to actually ride on the trailer where, at least, he had great personal interest in preventing runaways.

The other useful possibility was the semi-trailer, in which part of the load is supported by the rear axle of the hauling vehicle to form the combination known as the articulated, now found everywhere. Advantages are now seen as combining maximum carrying capacity, manoevrability, operational flexibility, and stability at speed with minimum length. When 'artics' first came into general use, during the early 1920s, more basic claims were made and the object then was to greatly increase the carrying capacity of vehicles intended to meet lesser demands: a common claim was that articulation gave 10 tonnes capacity at 3 tonnes cost. Most lorry chassis converted at that time suffered woeful abuse, although that was certainly not the case with many steam wagons that also were adapted for use as artics – most steamers were heavily over-engineered for their nominal carrying

Opposite: A smooth band of solid rubber offered little resistance to skids in any direction, and one chance encounter with a half-brick would ruin the whole tyre. Many palliatives were tried, including tyres assembled from separate blocks, but none were particularly successful.

While speeds were low there was no need at all for any refinement in trailer design – indeed, replacing shafts with a drawbar was all that was needed to convert a horse-drawn vehicle into a lorry trailer. Wooden brake blocks on the rearmost trailer wheels were pulled on by the driver's mate, using a cab-mounted winch. The wagon, an Allchin of about 1912, shows why some means of extending the load carrying capacity of overtype steamers was necessary.

Articulated lorries, with their two halves carefully matched for performance, are now in general use throughout the world. The idea of articulation is as old as the industry, but the first artic to be designed as a whole and put into general production was almost certainly the Scammell of 1922. It set a pattern the rest were to follow.

capacities or available body space and many gained new leases of life as very successful tractors for both drawbar and semi-trailers.

The foundations of the modern artic were laid in 1922 when Scammell built a new factory in the outskirts of London expressly to manufacture matched tractor semi-trailer outfits capable of handling the heaviest of contemporary loads. Other makers quickly followed suit, and by the mid-1920s articulated lorries for payloads from 1·5 to 12 tonnes abounded. Common sense—and steadily improving tyre quality—soon led to the abandon-

ment of the smallest sizes of artic, but operators were not slow to realise that, provided the travelling time involved was of suitable length, one tractor could easily keep three trailers busy. And since those were the years when a great many horses were being replaced, and since a motor can usually cover more ground than a horse in any given period of time, it followed that an articulated lorry would be much cheaper than animal traction. The main delay in use was the time it took to couple and uncouple the semi-trailer and designers quickly began to introduce a variety of high-speed couplers.

Scammell Six Wheeler
½ TONS at 3 Ton Cost & Speed.

Opposite and below: Whatever its disadvantages the horse-drawn vehicle was very manoeuvrable and rather small, so when the time came to replace it directly existing docksides and factory yards rapidly became cramped and congested with conventional motor lorries. The Mechanical Horse, suggested Scammell, was the answer: a simple three-wheeled tractor with an automatic coupling device that could pick up or drop small semi-trailers without the driver having to leave his cab. Each semi-trailer had a pair of support legs with flanged wheels; as the Horse backed under, the wheels rode up ramps and automatically folded the legs out of the way. Electrical and brake connexions were made at the same time. The whole process took just a few seconds.

Although not by any means the first, the best — almost without challenge — become the design known for many years as the Scammell 'Mechanical Horse'. Two versions were made, for 3 tonnes and 6 tonnes, and the equipment was mounted on suitable short wheelbase tractor chassis produced by most of the popular makers. Scammell itself produced odd-looking three-wheeled tractors that added extreme manoeuvrability to their other virtues. Chenard Walcker, who were Scammell concessionaires, produced very similar machines for the French market. In these combinations, both tractor and trailer were purpose-made. Karrier had the bright idea of producing a light tractor capable of coupling to a horse-drawn truck, but this was a short-lived expedient.

Without question, the main intention of those who adopted articulation was to increase carrying capacity at minimum expense, but a useful incidental advantage with the better conceived and engineered vehicles was that loads were spread over a greater number of wheels — and tyres. An equally obvious way of achieving the same result was to lengthen the chassis and body of a four-wheeled lorry and to put another axle under the extension. It was, however, an idea which lacked appeal during the solid tyred era, but six-wheelers became something of a craze in the late 1920s and chassis for loads as small as 1·5 tonnes had third axles added. Virtually all these later six-wheelers

and their modern descendants had rigid rear bogies, on which there is a measure of skidding when bends are negotiated. More refined designs were marketed during the first decade of the twentieth century by the French Lorraine Dietrich and Brillié companies, who both produced three-axle machines with the front and rearmost wheels arranged to steer. The idea has been revived in more recent times to ease the passage of long modern lorries.

PROGRESS UNLIMITED
1930-1960

A prerequisite of all lorries used until the early 1930s was the ability to withstand considerable overloading, a practice founded in the days of heavy, sturdy, slow vehicles; old habits lingered, and even lightweights like this American-inspired Bedford had to be capable of withstanding burdens well beyond their rated capacity.

By 1930 two momentous events in the history of heavy road transport had come to pass: one was the arrival and total acceptance of heavy duty pneumatic tyres; the other was a beginning to the end of spark ignition petrol engines.

In one sense the first was the more profound change, for although diesel engines did remarkable things for the economics of road transport, which was important, pneumatic tyres gave speed and endurance and forced the development of fast and reliable chassis. Long distance haulage ceased to be a thing of wonder and became an unremarkable everyday sort of business, and a rapidly proliferating one. It was obviously absurd to force this new kind of vehicle to observe legal speed limits that ten years before had been more that adequate for solid tyres, particularly as so many new or upgraded roads were already in

existence. At the same time, no responsible national government could stand aloof and permit the potential hazards – and there were many – in this new kind of transport to go unchecked.

In the flood of new and revised laws affecting transport in this period, those dealing with vehicle construction and use were to exercise the greatest long-term influence. During the 1920s the nominal capacity of a lorry was usually equivalent to its unladen weight, or even less. Manufacturers, however, expected their products to be grossly overloaded and even boasted about it: the General Motors Bedford range of trucks launched in the British Empire and elsewhere just as the new decade opened was guaranteed to accept 50 per cent excess of rated capacities; Ford, a year or two later, made similar promises. Meanwhile thousands of 3 and 4 tonne lorries surviving from

the First World War were regularly imposed upon to the extent of 5 or 6 tonnes or more – and they frequently hauled sizeable drawbar trailers into the bargain. So, with existing vehicles being grossly (and often dangerously) overloaded; with well surfaced new roads; with a new kind of vehicle already coming into service; and with a growing realisation by railway authorities that something dreadful was happening to their receipts, the climate was ripe for change and control. The result, taking a long-term view and with the benefit of hindsight, was almost entirely beneficial to the cause of road transport, although to judge by the widespread outcry from lorrymen of the time few had the foresight and forbearance to recognise it as such; but then, a great many of them were about to be put out of business.

Many countries introduced rates of annual taxation based on unladen weight, and coupled them with maximum speed limits, the whole calculated to encourage development of chassis capable of running at comparatively high speeds in safety, while causing minimum damage to road surfaces and foundations. The plan worked: within a few years the old, heavy, slow, solid-tyred lorries had all trundled into breakers' yards, their places filled by vehicles designed to fit the new taxation-weight categories. By the mid-1930s, far from offering unladen weight-to-payload ratios of 1:1, manufacturers had to do better than 1:2 if they and their customers were to survive. Their joint problems were not eased by a new insistence, rigidly enforced in most settled countries and firmly maintained still, that rated capacities must not be exceeded. A prime cause of this concern was the unwillingness of pneumatic tyres to accept the abuse that solids took uncomplainingly; another was the spectacular damage that could result from an overloaded lorry crashing at the new high speeds, and the resultant unflattering public comment about legislators who allowed such things to happen. Whatever the underlying causes, however, not a few firms on both sides of the industry failed during those turbulent years of the early 1930s, victims of their own inability to adjust quickly enough to an entirely different way of life.

The difficult economic climate of those years, coupled with the inescapable fact that road transport as a whole was seeking to squeeze its way into an already adequately served market, and that users were compelled to pay higher prices for (much better) vehicles, not to mention expensive petrol, all helped persuade European buyers to adopt diesel engines and the benefits of lower running costs offered by the new power units more readily than might otherwise have been the case. In Britain, the switch was further encouraged by the coincidental demise of road steamers, accidentally killed off by changes in the law. There were said to be just 90 diesel powered vehicles on British roads in 1930: five years later the figure was rapidly approaching 11,000; although the latter figure included buses, it was still a very remarkable transformation. In France, the diesel was seized upon with relief, for the authorities there had long been worried about their limited access to petrol.

French manufacturers rapidly turned to diesel power, showing in the process a marked ability for original thought. Two-stroke engines were for some years a constant theme, and beneath a conventional bonnet this Morton of 1929 housed a vertical four-cylinder two-stroke with poppet valves in its head. The Morton also had a 'dead' rear axle with separate drive shafts – and the rear wheels were cambered in order to load the twin tyres evenly.

Many engineers sought engines capable of burning oil fuels without the need for an ignition system, but it was Dr Rudolf Diesel who succeeded in getting his name accepted as the generic one for all engines of this kind.

Early oilers were slow, heavy, and not easy to start: before the type could become the all-conquering force which it now is, all three drawbacks had to be overcome – together with a fourth: price. Frank Perkins was not an innovator, except in one sense: he mass-produced diesels of capacities and dimensions that made it possible to fit them into chassis designed for petrol engines. And the cost of installation and running was right, too. Perkins is leaning on his 100,000th engine, back in 1952.

That was why French engineers spent so much time and trouble seeking to develop battery-electric and producer-gas alternatives, but these (and other) unsatisfactory expedients were all but dropped when the apparently multi-fuel diesel came upon the scene. In the oil-rich America of the 1930s fuel costs were of less importance and big petrol engines for lorries and buses held almost universal sway until very recently, 30 years or more after their virtual extinction in Europe.

Considerable debate surrounds the origins of the oil engine and the identities of the individuals who deserve credit for its development; indeed, until very recent times there was much debate on the propriety of naming it after Doctor Diesel, who is widely held to have done little to deserve the honour. In truth, however, so many men in so many places helped the oiler to become a useful source of power for road vehicles that no one person or company may fairly claim to have done more than any other. In the context of engines for road vehicles, it is sufficient to say that at the beginning of the 1920s the nearest thing to a suitable unit was too slow, too heavy, produced insufficient power and was unstartable by road vehicle standards; and that ten years later, thoroughly acceptable engines of a radically different kind were being produced

and installed by the thousand. Germany took the lead in forcing this remarkable rate of development, closely followed by Britain. In the latter a somewhat bizarre chain of events led to some government interest and money being expended on oil engine design as part of an overall and generally unsuccessful attempt to produce a large, safe, hydrogen-filled airship. As it happened, diesel engines and aircraft were never really to mix, but road transport at least gained something from the attempt.

Other far-reaching and enduring developments took place at much the same time, nearly all of them seeking to improve vehicle capacity since speed, the other obvious way of improving overall efficiency, was strictly controlled by law. Two distinct trends became apparent during the years between about 1930 and 1960: Europe came to favour large, often multi-axled load carriers, frequently hauling separate drawbar trailers; America leaned towards articulateds for its maximum capacity long haul transport. America is still a land of large articulated trucks, but Europe has made great strides in the same direction during the last 30 years while still keeping much of its earlier affection for the drawbar trailer.

A marked development during the 1930s – if development is the right word – was the virtual extinction of original thought on the grand scale in vehicle design. The pioneering, adventurous days in manufacturers' drawing offices drew to a close with the general adoption of the pneumatic tyre, that great milestone; the generally uneasy years between 1930 and 1940 were years of increasing consolidation both in design and among makers.

The lorry of the 1920s was essentially a four-wheeler (which remains, of course, numerically the most important single category); but one of the things which has added a great deal to the interest in lorries has been the great and continuing preoccupation during succeeding decades with multi-wheeled designs.

Many a four-wheeled chassis had its carrying capacity abruptly raised by the simple expedient of adding a trailing axle. Most such conversions were very simple indeed – at least this Ford gained a measure of articulation for its rear axles while being transformed from a 1 to a 1·5 tonner. No additional braking was thought necessary.

Ford, like its customers, realised that there was unrealised potential in the cheap but tough components it produced. One of many results was a properly engineered rigid six-wheeler, with double drive and braking on all wheels. Single tyres probably indicate user preference for increased body length rather than weight capacity.

It was natural enough to mount another axle immediately behind the existing drive axle to increase considerably both cargo space and payload, and as the 1920s wore on a considerable number of vehicles were thus equipped, either by conversion specialists who adapted existing (and often unsuitable) four-wheelers, or by manufacturers keen to enlarge the range of their wares at a minimum outlay. These makeshift six-wheelers served after a fashion but hardly any were integral designs, and the components from which they were assembled had only just been capable of coping with the demands imposed on them in four-wheeled guise.

Once again pneumatic tyres were the catalyst: in their more primitive forms it was generally deemed unwise to impose much of a load on those at the rear of a vehicle, since they already had to cope with the stresses of transmitting engine power to the road and, in those days of two-wheel brakes, all the strain of stopping the vehicle. On the other hand, tyres had to be so large in cross-section that it was impossible to mount them in pairs (as later became near-universal practice) and still keep within legally imposed restrictions on vehicle widths. Even if they had been so mounted, the confined environment would probably have led to sufficient heat build-up to destroy the rubber compounds of the day.

The answer was simple: add another driven axle and at once both problems were overcome. With the greater ability of pneumatics to yield to sideways forces when negotiating bends, even steering was lighter than might have been expected, and the tyres also helped mollify road maintenance authorities, who were becoming concerned at the damage to paved surfaces caused by unyielding solid rubber tyres whenever the early six-wheelers skidded sideways.

Busmen all over the world seized on the new ideas with great enthusiasm, largely because they made possible a considerable increase in seating capacity; the useful predictability of bus operating conditions also helped make it possible for manufacturers and users to gain confidence. In the bus world there was, indeed, a 'half-generation' of vehicles riding on air but owing much to solid-tyred designs of the early 1920s. Lorry users waited, on the whole, for the new generation – new from front to back, that is – of vehicles which came on to the market after 1930. In any case, freight carriers already had a very different kind of six-wheeler, the articulated, which could easily provide more load-carrying space than any rigid chassis, combined with a highly desirable degree of operating flexibility.

Given the rigid six-wheeler, it was only a matter of time, in those countries where construction and use regulations could be interpreted so as to give a payload advantage, before a rigid eight bowed in. At once it gave payload capacity, enough tyres to distribute loadings evenly on to the road, ample braking capacity, and a combination of surefootedness and directional stability that was hard to equal. Even when the necessarily restricted length of the load platform was a hindrance, a better towing vehicle for separate drawbar trailers could hardly be found. It is in many ways a great pity that the rigid eight is now so thoroughly overshadowed

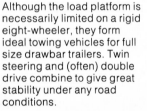

Although the load platform is necessarily limited on a rigid eight-wheeler, they form ideal towing vehicles for full size drawbar trailers. Twin steering and (often) double drive combine to give great stability under any road conditions.

Two reasons for twin-steer six-wheelers. Several operators engaged in urban delivery work have adopted twin steering on Ford and other chassis *(above)* in order to get a low platform height. Less than standard-sized wheels and tyres would incur a weight penalty: the extra axle restores capacity. The Hanomag Henschel articulated tractor *(left)* has an extra axle so that semi-trailers of certain configurations will not impose too much weight on the rearmost, driving, axle.

by articulation, which can achieve similar levels of stability only with great difficulty.

No one adds the complication, cost and weight of an extra axle merely for the look of the thing, and although two axles at the rear certainly offer useful extra load-carrying capacity, the axle itself, whether driven or trailing, is heavy. If driven, there are mechanical complications in making sure each of the four wheels does its fair share of the work; if it trails, the unsophisticated suspensions of the

Occasionally users need a self-propelled very low platform lorry sufficiently to make the expense and trouble of getting one worth while. The obvious source of suitable components is a four-wheel drive vehicle, for it then becomes a relatively simple matter to take the front end complete – and thereby add to the bare handful of front-wheel drive lorries that have been made. This is an FWD of 1929, but several makes have undergone similar transformations over the years.

Opposite, top and bottom: Kenworth, in the United States, explored an interesting and attractive version of the rigid eight-wheeler during the latter 1950s. It had a flat engine, which helped keep cab length to a minimum and body length to a maximum, and it was arranged to run with a matched semi-trailer which pivoted over the drive axles.

1930s could make it difficult to fairly divide imposed loads while at the same time putting enough weight on the two driven wheels to give them bite on the road surface. There is another less obvious problem: on a conventional long wheelbase rigid six the extra capacity for weight is mainly at the back, and even with the cargo spread uniformly it is quite easy to put too much weight on to the front axle. It took until nearly the end of the decade before the obvious solution evolved: add the third axle at the front and make it steer – an arrangement which, in its definitive form, was pioneered by the British ERF and Fodens companies. Calculating weight dispositions and their effects is a subtle art, but this kind of chassis arrangement gave, broadly speaking, four tyres under each end of the load, instead of two at one end and eight at the other, with a certainty of steering that was unrivalled.

The remaining possibility, that of emulating so many makers of modern passenger cars and adopting front-wheel drive, was never seriously considered for heavy lorries, mainly because of the mechanical complexity of the resulting front axle and the difficulty of ensuring enough weight being placed over the driving wheels for adhesion. Even so a few heavy front-wheel drive lorries have been made over the years: Latil, without whom any account of vehicle design would be a dull affair, made some ultra-low-platform machinery carriers driven from the front, and in more recent times one of the English electricity authorities used the front halves of four-wheel drive Bedfords and Land-Rovers as the bases of cable drum carriers which also had very low frames.

It was weight distribution as much as anything which caused so much agonising during the 1930s about the relative positions of engine and driver's cab. The engine should be at the front of the vehicle, it was commonly agreed, for this freed the rear axle for payload. Yet in commercial vehicles, where body volume is usually of great importance (but not always – there are iron bars to be carried as well as corn flakes) it was manifestly absurd to follow passenger car practice and place the driver behind his power unit. Not only was a metre or more of overall length wasted on the engine, but

the sin was usually compounded by giving the driver a cab extending over the full vehicle width. One reason was maintenance; the engines of the first three decades of the twentieth century needed frequent maintenance and adjustment, and the few makers who attempted to popularise forward control, or cab-over, designs lived to rue it. Motoring fashion no doubt played its part, for those were the years when the very epitome of fashion in motor cars was a long rakish bonnet, and most lorry-owners were first-generation hauliers, whose emotions could still be stirred by the excitement of motoring. Even so, heavier lorry chassis soon began to follow bus design, which usually placed the driver alongside his engine and overcame servicing problems by adopting a half-width cab and arranging engine auxiliaries on the side most readily exposed. Lorries in those days usually carried a crew of two, so full-width cabs were the norm. Sadly frequent, too, were the curses of maintenance staff as they struggled to work (through a cab door) on engines that could not be reached while standing on the ground, and which (while working inside the cab) demanded a degree of bodily suppleness uncommon in most workshop men. Quite soon the problems of inaccessability became insignificant, for diesel engine reliability improved to the point where power units needed virtually no adjustment for weeks on end.

In the meantime some manufacturers, notably in Germany, threw to the wind any pretensions to grace or beauty in their products, with designs that combined an exposed engine compartment with a front axle set back under the cab. This arrangement helped not at all the problem of overall length, but engine accessibility was superb, crews had quiet and spacious working surroundings, turning circles could be small and the front axle was more easily given its fair share of weight.

Once Robert Bosch had perfected his jerk pump, and thus made it possible to inject tiny quantities of fuel oil into a cylinderful of very hot air, the so-called diesel engine became inevitable and highly attractive. Granted, it weighed a lot more than a petrol unit of equivalent power and it had to run more slowly, which meant that in any straightforward substitution into an erstwhile petrol-powered chassis, road speeds would also be lower. Diesel engines cost more, too, but the true price (before government-imposed tax) of the light oil used for fuel is about half that of petrol, while a tankful may well take a lorry twice as far as petrol, so that such drawbacks as there were soon faded into insignificance.

Right from the beginning diesel engines intended for road use adopted the format of most petrol engines and this is still the case today. At first four cylinders in line working on the four-stroke principle were the norm, but most manufacturers rapidly produced a straight six, which remains the most popular configuration today. Only three major deviations from this conformity can be said to have achieved real commercial success: the great family of two-strokes produced over the last 40 or so years by the Detroit Diesel subsidiary of General Motors; air cooling, brought to a fine art by Magirus-Deutz in the years after the Second World War, despite the maker's earlier commitment to radiators and water pumps; and, finally, a leaning by some engine makers during the last two decades towards vee-formation cylinders. This latter arrangement offers either increased power within existing space limitations or less bulk for the same output, so it is very attractive to chassis designers struggling to instal engines producing sufficient power to meet modern legal and operational requirements into chassis frames that are not much wider or longer than their predecessors of ten and 20 years ago.

Both two-strokes and air cooling have lasted a long time and meet one criteria of engineering success: customers not only continue to buy them, but they do so in sufficient numbers to warrant regular updating and redesigns. But the other measure of success, that of general adoption by rival makers, has not been met—and the few

Determined to combine the engine accessibility of normal control chassis with the turning circle and cab comfort of the cab-over, many makers dabbled with arrangements like this Büssing of 1931. Within a few years, however, improved reliability reduced the need for easy access and legal restrictions on dimensions discouraged unnecessary length.

tentative steps taken in that direction, either quite independently or in imitation, have come to nothing. The German Junkers concern was an early adventurer into the apparent attractions of two-stroke diesels, but made the fatal error of concealing within conventional exteriors a mechanical arrangement that might have been calculated to frighten any owner or mechanic whose experience was limited to road vehicles.

In the Junkers, each vertical cylinder contained two pistons, with the upper one acting as an air pump and covering and uncovering cylinder-wall

inlet ports, while the lower piston performed the same function for the exhaust ports and turned the crankshaft. The French Compagnie Lilloise de Moteurs was probably the most enthusiastic propounder of the Junkers gospel: it produced a single-cylinder unit that Lavigne installed in a 1 tonne capacity chassis, and a two-cylinder version that it managed to sell to Willème, Peugeot, Laffly and Bernard, among others. (Peugeot, in fact, deserves its own niche in the two-stroke hall of fame for, very soon after the First World War ended, the company produced a two-stroke diesel

Deutz bravely adopted the then-unfashionable format of air-cooled vee engines during the late 1940s and has persevered with it ever since. Now the company has a highly rationalised range of power units for all kinds of purposes: they share many common components and have proved highly acceptable in marine, industrial, and automotive applications.

for vehicle use. This relied upon an external heat source to achieve working temperatures; the project found little interest.)

A three-cylinder Junkers design made by Lilloise and tried by Willème was rated to produce 80 hp at 1,500 rpm; it weighed about 450 kg, and none of those figures were anything to be ashamed of in 1931. Miesse in Belgium and Gilford in England also experimented with these extraordinary engines: within a year or two Miesse turned to solidly conventional and reliable Gardner products and Gilford became bankrupt — not entirely, it must be said, through trying a two-stroke diesel engine, but at least in part because of the equally strange front-wheel drive double-deck bus in which it was installed.

The old-established English firm of Fodens — which may indeed be the oldest maker of commercial vehicles in the world — was also lured into

spending a great deal of time and money during the 1940s and 1950s trying to develop a two-stroke capable of equalling a four-stroke in economy and reliability. Ultimately Fodens succeeded, just in time to be overtaken by newly increased permissable vehicle weights and dimensions that were beyond the capabilities of its engine. The company gave up its only attempt to build its own power units and returned to proprietary engines, although the two-stroke found wide application in its marinised versions.

It is a tantalising thing, the two-stroke. In theory it should be half the size of a four-stroke and much lighter, while its promise of a power impulse on every downstroke instead of only on every alternate stroke is self-evidently attractive and should mean only half the number of cylinders. Sadly, as any engineer knows, simplicity can usually be obtained only from much complexity and the prob-

For its only attempt to build an engine of its own Fodens also turned to the two-stroke principle, and contrived to get impressively high power outputs from light, small units. Sustained reliability under automotive operating conditions proved elusive, however, and although ultimately successful the engine was outpaced by increases in permitted vehicle weights and dimensions.

The Rootes two-stroke was a 'flat' engine with three cylinders and six pistons. Despite being so much out of the general run of vehicle engine design it was reliable and well-liked, and lent itself well to multi-fuel adaptations for military purposes. It, too, was overtaken by vehicle legislation, its makers preferring not to invest further in designing and developing larger versions.

lems of getting fuel into each cylinder, then burnt thoroughly in the available time, and then cleanly exhausted – all in one stroke – are very real. And when legislators throughout the world began to take an interest in controlling noise and exhaust emissions, vehicle designers, sensibly if unadventurously, turned to familiar principles, and engines.

Another dead-end in the diesel story during the early 1930s was the sleeve-valve design produced in four and six cylinder forms by Panhard et Levassor. That Panhard took up the idea in the first place was surprising, for sleeve valves were already obsolete for automotive use, even among the few makers who had adopted them for the less difficult circumstances of petrol-burning engines. Sleeve-valve engines had inlet and outlet ports cut in the cylinder walls – rather like a two-stroke – and these ports were systematically covered and uncovered by sleeves with corresponding ports, which slid up and down the cylinders. Originally the idea was an American one, but it was adopted with great enthusiasm by the Belgian Minerva and British Daimler concerns, who brought petrol sleeve-valve engines to a fine state of perfection and used them extensively in large cars, buses and lorries; Minerva, too, made a diesel sleeve valve. By 1931, however, the chief virtue of sleeve-valve engines, an absence of mechanical noise, was being overtaken by ordinary power units using new materials and techniques in their valve operating gears, and poppet valves were already assuming the virtually unchallenged role they have held ever since.

Remembering the great suspicion and caution with which unconventional engines are regarded by makers and users alike, the British-made Rootes engine of the late 1940s should have been a first-rate recipe for disaster. Not only was it a two-stroke with six pistons working in only three cylinders, but it had a flat formation and lived under the cab floor. In this extraordinary power unit the piston crowns faced each other and fuel burned between them. The mechanical complexity necessary to link the connecting rods to a common crankshaft was reminiscent of the sort of thing perpetrated in the earliest days of motor engineer-

ing, but the whole worked very well indeed. There could easily have been a four cylinder version capable of producing enough power to meet most modern requirements, and it was unfortunate that changes in both company fortunes and the British Construction and Use laws coincided to hasten its demise. Many Rootes two-strokes were installed in chassis bearing the once-familiar name of Commer and the remarkable sound emitted by them was quite distinct from any of their conventionally powered contemporaries.

The flat format engine should be near-ideal for most kinds of heavy lorry, for it at once frees the cab from obstruction and noise, provides easy accessibility for servicing and removal, and allows the heavy unit weight of the engine to be positioned to best advantage anywhere along the chassis frame. Although flat engines became near-universal for heavier single-deck buses during the 1950s and 1960s, however, and are significant still in that sphere of commercial vehicle endeavour, only the German Büssing concern and Sentinel in England adopted underfloor-engined lorries with any enthusiasm. An interesting point is that virtually all the power units used flat were ordinary vertical engines laid on their sides, and modified to a greater or lesser degree for their new role. One result was certainly the increased cylinder wear to which many were prone, along with recurrent lubrication problems: mere rumour of such potential ailments would be more than enough to deter the average buyer of lorries. Yet Büssing customers thought so highly of their lorries that when, some years later, the company were absorbed into MAN, so many users insisted on horizontally-engined chassis that it was commercially possible to make and supply them.

But such interesting deviations from the norm were becoming rare as the 1950s wore to a close. Pressures of every kind were bearing on manufacturers and many had soon to give up control of their destinies. Uniformity certainly has its virtues, but it takes a great deal away from the pleasures of visiting the big commercial vehicle exhibitions, or of exploring a roadside truck stop – or even just of standing by the roadside watching lorries roll by. . .

Mounting the engine flat under the chassis of a lorry should give maximum freedom for arranging the cab and bodywork, while at the same time offering good accessibility to the unit itself. Although popular for buses, however, flat engines have not aroused much enthusiasm among truck users, except among those who used to buy Büssing, and who now insist that MAN (Büssing successors) still provide underfloor engined lorries.

MODERN TIMES

Opposite: Modern-day truck building is an international affair . . . American owned Ford assembles its British-designed Transcontinentals in The Netherlands, from components produced by companies which also operate on a world-wide basis. Like several of its competitors, Ford finds itself having to buy in material from rival firms – in this case cabs from Berliet-Renault.

Following colour pages: For many years the isolation that afflicted Spain kept its vehicle designers away from the mainstream of design. One result was the spectacularly styled products of Pegaso, quite unmistakable and guaranteed to turn heads wherever they ventured across frontiers on TIR work.

The American-based General Motors Corporation owns Bedford and Opel in Europe and sells Japanese Isuzu trucks throughout the world; Iveco comprises Fiat, OM and Lancia in Italy, Magirus Deutz in Germany, and Unic in France; Sweden's Volvo is involved in a joint development project with Magirus Deutz, Saviem (France) and DAF (Holland); International, from the US, owns a piece of DAF and Pegaso, all of the British Seddon Atkinson concern, and licenses the Mexican Dina.

Saviem, linked in recent times with fellow-national Berliet, now sells in most countries as Renault and has common production arrangements with MAN from Germany; Berliet supplies cabs to Ford in Europe; MAN licences a Hungarian factory to build and market its designs as Raba, a Rumanian factory to produce Romans, it cross-trades with the Austrian OAF concern, and has joined forces with Volkswagen to develop a range of trucks. Peugeot (France) has acquired the Chrysler Europe business and with it the Barreiros, Commer and Dodge labels, and explores research projects with DAF. Kenworth, Dart, Peterbilt – the list is seemingly endless. . . .

The tangle of links, cross-links, joint agreements, and mutual parts-sourcing that form the world-wide commercial vehicle building industry is now so intricately woven that any attempt to unravel it or to compile an overall family tree would sink under the sheer weight of its own complexity. Clearly the technical and financial independence that was once the proud boast of many commercial vehicle makers is rapidly becoming a thing of the past. After all, to develop an entirely new diesel engine – and the tooling to make it – might easily cost in the region of £200 million; a brand new gearbox would cost perhaps half as much. It is easy to see why nearly all heavy chassis makers use combinations of products by the same handful of familiar names: engines from Cummins, Perkins, Rolls-Royce, Detroit, Caterpillar or Gardner; transmissions from ZF, Fuller, Allison or David Brown; axles from Eaton, Kirkstall or Rockwell.

And it is easy to see why much of the traditional brand loyalty from customers has ebbed away. When similar combinations of components produce similar performances, buying decisions are more than ever made on a careful evaluation of price, discounts, financial accommodations and, above all, the quality of after-sales spares and service facilities. In a real sense, buyers have turned the old loyalty to makers into loyalty to dealers. Should a dealer transfer his allegiance from one factory to another (and the spate of post-1960 mergers and takeovers has forced a great many retail outlets to find new wares to sell) he will, in all probability, take with him many of his old customers.

More than any other single factor this instability of loyalty has made possible the tremendous growth of international marketing of heavy commercial vehicles during the last two decades. Many a dealer, who once would never have considered selling anything but the products of his fellow nationals, is now glad to be given a chance to handle alien makes. Since the first essential of any sales campaign is a good network of properly staffed and equipped service depots, the way is automatically, if coincidentally, opened to long-distance international haulage.

After a few years, a firm which started out as an alien importer increases the local content of its products, begins local assembly, and becomes to some degree naturalised. This is a sequence of events heartily encouraged by many governments, particularly in 'third world' countries, where the tendency is to encourage unrestricted imports for a while and then, by means of controls and taxation, to virtually compel the lorry maker to use an increasing proportion of locally produced components. It is a useful ploy in any country struggling to reduce its foreign exchange problems, and at the same time it creates a pool of skilled labour. A remarkable recent example is Nigeria, where state-backed contracts have led British Leyland, Austrian Steyr, German Mercedes and Italian Fiat to build large plants. Initially, assembly from kits sent from the home factories will predominate, but within a few years most of each vehicle will be made locally. Scania, aware of the political realities of life for an exporter based in a small neutral country, has established virtually autonomous factories in Brazil and Argentina; fellow national Volvo, recognising its largest single market, has equipped a large plant in Britain to build and modify vehicles for local customers – and has constructed a plant in Brazil.

Because of the enormous investment required to put new designs into production, component makers must be even more multi-national. Perhaps the record-holder is the Canadian-owned but British-based Perkins Engines concern: it makes diesel power units in France, India, Spain, Brazil, Argentina and Italy and has facilities elsewhere to completely re-manufacture worn engines. Eaton

Following colour pages:
Haulage, traditional style.
The driver, and perhaps his
mate, have spent a long time
carefully sheeting and
roping the load on the flat-
bed Bedford, and are no
doubt taking one of the rest
breaks compelled upon
them by law. Soon the diesel
will growl into life, the lights
will be switched on, and
another long and uneventful
journey will begin. It is a fine
night: by dawn they may be
hundreds of kilometers
away.

The days are now long gone
when chassis makers could
dismiss the matter of
supplying a cab as a matter
for someone else to worry
about. Gone too are the
days when any sort of shed
would serve: now a lorry cab
must be nearly as elaborate
in structure and trim as a
passenger car, and almost
as expensive to produce.
Co-operation is one answer,
and careful examination of
the cabs fitted to this ERF
(right), Seddon *(below),* Guy
(opposite, top), and Floor
(opposite bottom), shows
that they share several
major components
produced by specialists
Motor Panels.

Corporation, whose axles and Fuller gearboxes are common currency, has factories in America, Britain, and France.

In almost all these commercial developments — and in most technical ones, for that matter — there is no doubt that the Western European makers

have dominated. In cut-throat competition with each other, they have colonised the uncommitted world, while some of them are now devoting considerable time and money to denting the domination by American makers of their home market. Apart from General Motors and Ford (which both have truck-building factories in several overseas countries), the Americans have shown surprisingly little interest in exporting heavy chassis, such sales as they have made being mainly to places like Australia and South Africa, where conditions can be much like those in the States. Eastern European factories, relying heavily on technology leased from the West, have been almost fully occupied in meeting home demands, while Japanese makers have yet to begin the kind of all-conquering effort that has taken their cars and light vans all over the world — which is not to suggest that they cannot or will not once they judge that the time is right. . . .

Although there is not much apparent difference between the heavy vehicles built during the 1950s and their latter-day descendants, very few components would really be interchangeable. Although many current engine designs first saw the light of day two decades or more ago, constant refinement has produced power outputs and fuel consumption that would have been scarcely credible when the first versions of those engines were put to work. Equally unbelievable in 1950 would have been the life spans and servicing intervals that are part of modern engine economics, and much the same is true of the drive train, steering, brakes and other components.

None of these marvels would be possible, of course, were it not for the great strides in materials

Turkey, a country needing simple and robust trucks, invited Leyland to collaborate in establishing a factory. Using a well-established medium weight design as a basis, the quantity of locally produced components has steadily risen: the need for expensive and complicated press tool work was obviated by adopting this simple though good-looking flat sheet cab.

An apparently insatiable home market deterred most American makers from major efforts at exporting until more recent times. Now useful volumes of sales are being generated in such places as Australia, South Africa, and the Middle East, and unmistakably American trucks like this Mack are to be met on European roads.

technology and research. When the quantities required are low, even a simple bracket may have to be made as a casting in the age-old manner; increase the number of parts and sophisticated steel forgings – lighter, more durable, better looking, and produced on highly automated equipment – became economically possible. Even when castings are still desirable, for such things as brake drums, cylinder liners and bearing bushes, it is economically possible to move away from the old gravity casting manufacturing processes, with their uncertain quality, to centrifugal castings, where the molten metal is spun into precision moulds to form units that will perform predictably throughout a very long life.

By moving away from the time-honoured strip-type brake linings to the now-universal moulded and bonded form, makers gained materials more easily compounded to meet their precise requirements – and a useful increase in friction area, simply by deleting the securing rivets. That other essential friction device, the clutch, also had to be improved as increasing engine and vehicle size and speed took it to the limits of its abilities. But chassis makers did not need to rely on their own resources for such things; specialist concerns soon

made available new designs, with twin plates in place of the old singles, some even forsaking the time-honoured asbestos lining for ceramics.

The march of technology has also left its mark on the tyres used by heavy commercial vehicles. It was a long time before the radial revolution – which, led by Michelin, swept the passenger car business during the 1960s – made much impression on the lorry industry, at least partly due to the understandable conservatism of men whose livelihoods literally depend upon tyres. Higher initial cost was no encouragement, but the evidence soon showed that radials enjoyed a much longer life, lower rolling resistance and brought fuel savings of perhaps ten per cent, not to mention a reduction in unsprung weight of around 20 kg compared with older cross-ply casings (20 kg may not seem a great deal, until it is remembered that an ordinary articulated lorry has 14 tyres). One result of the consequent rise in radial usage is that tyre makers have found their sales dropping dramatically, adding to their similar problems in the passenger car trade.

Even the chassis frame, which does not really seem susceptible to much change, has benefited greatly from the ready availability of better materials for those who can use large enough quantities

By dint of much cutting and welding, York Trailer contrives to reduce the unladen weight of its semi-trailer frames to a minimum. The main chassis members are really H-section joists, but by profiling them and rejoining the pieces the so-called 'castellated' frame emerges, to offer considerable rigidity. Light section cross members are passed through holes pierced in the main members, again in the interests of stiffness without avoidable weight.

The days are long gone when operators could afford the cost and time that it took to paint and decorate a lorry. Now just one day off the road is a serious matter, and manufacturers are expected to turn out their products finish-painted all but for the owners name, which is simply stripped in with a self-adhesive plastics overlay. The old Albion *(far left, upper)* shows how things were done once; a Volvo and matching semi-trailer *(below)* illustrate how effective a simple, easily applied livery can be. Another Volvo *(above)* and the Bedford *(above, left)* re-emphasise the point. Indeed, the few examples of old-time elaboration that can still be found almost invariably sit uncomfortably on the smooth lines of modern cabs.

Although some cynics might dispute it, the days are long gone when manufacturers could leave much of the post-production development of their vehicles to customers. Unfortunately this introduces a difficult problem: how else can a machine demonstrate its ability to work without breakdowns over a full life-span without actually doing so? An enormous amount of time and money is therefore spent in devising and executing testing procedures that accelerate wear and failure. Every prototype will most certainly have to cover huge distances in endurance running both at high speed on private tracks and under something akin to regular conditions on public roads. The two Austins of 1964 *(top)* were in the throes of an 80,000 km run, completed virtually non-stop at 80 km/h, fully laden. If the weather is a hazard to operators it is doubly so for testers – for they have to prove that their vehicles can cope with anything they are likely to meet. These Russian drivers *(centre)* clearly had no difficulty in finding low temperature conditions for their Kamaz chassis: the crash helmets underline the considerable risks inherent in pushing heavy vehicles to the limits of their performance. One of the strangest experiences is to stand in an anachoic chamber: every sound is absorbed by the special wall padding – there are no echoes. But these eerie places form ideal surroundings in which to measure the variety of noises emitted by engines and other components. The Perkins Engine company has carried out a great deal of fundamental research into noise in its anachoic rooms *(bottom, left)*. Inside the framework *(bottom, right)* is a Ford cab undergoing 160 km of rough roads every five minutes. Hydraulic rams, tape controlled, apply the loadings.

A contrast which shows clearly why victory in the battle for sales inevitably goes to the biggest battalions. Just four decades ago it was possible for Thornycroft to competitively market a wide range of vehicles on world markets, despite using a great deal of hand labour to produce a high quality product *(above)*. Now the highly automated production line has taken over almost completely, and Daimler Benz, *(left)* one of many, can build hundreds of high quality chassis where once-traditional methods could have made only dozens.

An inescapable part of the modern road transport industry is the need for very large, heavily capitalised, vehicle distributors and dealers who have made big investments in diagnostic and repair workshops. Only the biggest vehicle owners can sensibly equip themselves to carry out major servicing and repair work.

Refinement of vehicle performance entails vastly more complicated machines than those of even 20 or 30 years ago. And although servicing intervals are also much extended workshop labour is now so expensive that quick and ready access to everything likely to need attention is vital. The Scania *(above)* is an example of how most makers provide for frequent checks, like oil and water levels; the Magirus *(opposite)* shows not only how useful a tilt cab can be, but also how neatly the makers have installed a V12 engine producing 340 bhp beneath the driver's feet.

have access to large test tracks on which experimental vehicles can cover huge distances under simulated road conditions – and, of course, where there are lengths of impossibly rough surfaces, hills, watersplashes, and other obstacles calculated to ensure that any potential component failures are discovered before production vehicles get into customers' hands.

Equally impressive are the test cells, replete with electronic instrumentation, in which an engine, gearbox or axle can run its allotted life span and beyond without even seeing a vehicle. Every part is overloaded and overheated, its behaviour minutely observed and recorded, so that the durability of each is finely tuned to make a predictable whole; for predictability of performance is most desirable in these days of high maintenance and downtime costs. The same kind of detached thoroughness is brought to bear on chassis frames, cabs and cab components – indeed, on every part of a modern vehicle. There is really no way in which these processes can be circumvented (except by using components proved by someone else) and the enormous cost in time and money of modern research does much to explain why victory in the mass markets is going, inevitably, to the largest companies.

The virtues of size do not end with manufacturers: their distributors must also be big enough to service and maintain large vehicles quickly and efficiently. In terms of capital invested and turnover, large distributor networks can easily rival small motor manufacturers. They need to be big: quite apart from the investment required to provide large premises strategically placed in the prime locations, the refinement of vehicle design is more than matched by advances in the equipment needed to keep the lorries operating efficiently. Air compressors, pressure washers, power greasers, hoists, rolling road brake testers and more – a modern servicing bay is not unlike an assembly line, except that the vehicles are grimier. The next big step will be the introduction of sophisticated plug-in diagnostic equipment of the kind already used for some passenger cars, where computers analyse the functioning of the mechanical vitals and recommend the treatment needed to restore them to health.

Such refinements are not, unfortunately, suitable for the many less advanced overseas markets, although it must be reassuring for vehicle makers to see that their products can withstand a degree of abuse and neglect unheard of in gentler climates. The apparent paradox of generally similar chassis giving satisfaction under such different conditions can largely be explained by the high wages and costs, and rigorously applied regulations of one sphere, and by a much reduced insistence on overall efficiency in the other.

A major area in which the computer is proving particularly useful is that of warehousing and distribution, which is now something of a science. Long truck runs are not difficult to plan and with the cargo in containers drivers need hardly leave their cabs. But the vast majority of journeys are very much shorter and involve several collection and delivery points on each journey. When vehicles were small – and in the days before the maze of

of them. Ford claims its Transcontinental frame is so tough as to be virtually undrillable – which seems irrelevant until it is noticed how thin, spare and light this chassis is. It is a far cry from the standard steel section frames of long-ago, although York has most successfully adopted such material in forming the castellated supporting frames for its large semi-trailers; but a great deal of cutting and welding, using equipment unimagined by the pioneers, is needed to achieve these airy – more space than steel – structures.

Equally intriguing is a strictly limited renewal of interest in centre spine chassis by Mercedes and DAF, who have observed the heavy unit weights in crates of bottled drinks, and the labour involved in stacking and unloading conventional truck bodies. By adopting a centre spine layout the crate racks can be brought almost to ground level. Clearly there are few really new ideas, but there is a great deal of potential in road transport for adapting old ideas to solve new problems. Equally clearly, mass-production of heavy commercial vehicles is not the enemy of quality and choice that it is so often accused of being in other fields.

The development of modern lorries is a constant battle to lengthen vehicle life while allowing unladen weight to rise by the barest possible minimum; a remarkable outcome of this is the enormous investment that most manufacturers now make in research facilities. Nearly all of them now own or

waiting restrictions, no-entry streets, weight limitations, controls on drivers, working hours and all the other regulations that now beset road transport – an experienced traffic clerk was more than a match for the day-to-day problems. Probably an ex-driver, he would know his company and its customers and would make sure that each lorry was loaded and routed so that every consignment was accessible when the driver wanted it. Complications like the dates and times when a shop or factory might be unable to receive its goods were second nature to such men, who scarcely needed a map when deciding what routes their vehicles would take.

In those days small lorries delivered small consignments to small shops; now giant supermarkets and hypermarkets require huge consignments to arrive with almost clockwork precision in order not to clash with other deliveries and to keep warehousing to a minimum. Where urban deliveries of the old style survive, drivers can be hard pressed to unload in the limited time they are allowed to park in busy streets; it is often necessary to stop some distance away and manhandle loads to the shop door. Many factories, depending upon outside suppliers for components, rely implicitly upon carefully timed lorry arrivals to keep their production lines flowing smoothly. And all this is additionally hampered by the fact that state and local authorities constantly alter road and town layouts, make new restrictions and change transport law.

It has all become too much for human brains to handle, particularly since the old, slowly changing patterns have become very volatile indeed, with violent fluctuations in work patterns and operating conditions. Happily, salvation came with computers. It took some years for computing equipment and techniques to overcome the fully justified suspicion of their usefulness, and stories were legion of the bizarre instructions emitted by the electronic machines. One favourite concerned a beautifully constructed delivery route, perfect in every respect – except that it assumed lorries needed no bridge to cross a wide, deep and swift-flowing river. . . .

That sort of thing is nearly in the past; modern low-cost computing equipment now handles the incredibly complicated business of deciding production programmes, obtaining orders, arranging suitable warehousing, dispatch and transport, load planning, routeing, making deliveries, requesting and getting payment – all are reduced to pressing keys at a computer terminal and reading a printout. In its spare moments the computer can schedule vehicle maintenance intervals and calculate staff wages. Nor is there any sign of a limit in its potential for further development.

BODYWORK

Without doubt, the overwhelming dominance in freight transport achieved by road vehicles stems almost entirely from the flexibility and infinite variety of operation that is possible when the individual transport unit is at once as small and manoevrable as the lorry, while individual vehicles can easily be equipped to meet specific needs. Whatever the cargo, a lorry can be tailored precisely to carry and often to handle it.

The same could not be claimed for the horse-drawn wagon. In its role as handmaiden to rail the need for any degree of specialisation hardly existed, while the limited traction output of the horse made complicated and weighty vehicles unattractive. Since the same considerations influenced the first motor lorries, they too tended toward simplicity. Their common denominator was certainly the flat tray style of body, capable of transporting almost any cargo from flour or coal (in sacks) to small but heavy pieces of machinery. Hitch an equally flat drawbar trailer to a lorry and the result can carry twice as much cargo, or something as unwieldy as a ship's mast or a consignment of telegraph poles.

But completely open vehicles, although very useful indeed and still used by the thousand, offer no security against loss or weather. So van bodywork, the other main form of horse-drawn vehicle, was also grafted on to the new motorised vehicles and rapidly achieved pre-eminence for some sorts of cargo, generally the kind involving low unit weights, for the great drawback of enclosed bodywork is the limited access. It might be very desirable to house, say, flour in a fully enclosed vehicle but the men given the task of carrying sacks weighing 90 kg or so would much prefer to have them lowered into place with a crane. This theme of open versus closed bodies, free versus limited access, runs through the whole history of mechanical road transport and has led to the evolution of some fascinating alternatives.

The third main type of bodywork for goods carrying is the tanker, versions of which now carry increasing tonnages of a surprising variety of commodities. A few, very few, tankers were made for horse-drawn transport and in the main they carried water for specific purposes – although right at the end of the nineteenth century some were made for

No difficulty, with this early de Dion Bouton, in recognising the influence of horse-drawn wagons. Positioning the crew on top of the engine gave them virtually no protection at all from bad weather, although there is a folding hood of sorts mounted behind the seat.

carrying the newly-introduced petroleum-based lamp oils in bulk to retail outlets. These demands were so small that there was no need for much attention to be given to refining tank design, and most of them resembled nothing so much as a small boiler with a tap at the back, perched on a flat wagon.

If the scope for early body designers was limited so were the materials with which they had to work; indeed, the whole art and craft of bodymaking was carried over from the horse-drawn era. This was understandable, but it led to an interesting side-effect in that the superb hand craftsmanship appropriate to vehicles that were quite static in design and with a probable life span of half a century or more was quite out of place in a product where thinking progressed in leaps and bounds, and where any vehicle which lasted five years in service was regarded as an historic curiosity. Motor lorries vibrated, often alarmingly, something of which their horse-drawn predecessors could not be accused, and few things cause more damage to delicately wrought and jointed timbers. Despite the manifest unsuitability of traditional construction and styling, however, both persisted until the last human survivors of that earlier era had also departed from the scene, which may conveniently be dated at 1939, with the renewal of war in Europe. After that, more pressing considerations than elegant jointing and chamfers and multi-coat

paint finishes became apparent in motor transport.

Timber was for many years the main material available to coachbuilders. It is easily worked and elaborate machining facilities are not essential. It is strong in relation to its weight, and so wide is the variety of characteristics available to the bodybuilder who knows his tree species that it is possible to find a wood suitable for almost every purpose. Iron or steel reinforcements and fastenings are very suitable, and, providing the quantities required are not too great, any competent blacksmith can produce them cheaply enough.

Finally, linen and cotton fabrics played an important part for many years (and to some extent still do), usually in the form of tarpaulin sheets for covering loads on open platform lorries, but also as weather proofing on van roofs; fabric possessed a degree of flexibility that was most useful on the constantly moving bodywork of the day.

Passenger car – and bus – manufacturers turned to metal bodywork as quickly as they could, because of the ease with which self-supporting components like wings and large pieces of roof could be made with only a minimum of timber framing underneath, and, of course, the ease with which those large pieces of panelling could be shaped and styled. Bus makers needed sheet metal for somewhat different reasons: buses must perforce have fairly elaborate framing, and sheet metal, properly secured to wooden or metal fram-

Adding a few bentwood hoops to an ordinary dropside body, and stretching a canvas sheet over the resulting framework could make a useful van. The unusually deep radiator – and perhaps the unusually generous awning over the crew – show that this Lacre was destined for a warm climate. Indeed, it went to Ceylon.

In a startling demonstration of a means to achieve rapid discharge from a van semi-trailer, the rigidity of construction that can come from using corrugated sheet panelling is also displayed. No separate chassis is fitted under the van, although the floor itself has stiffeners and the running gear needs a pair of girders. The Bartlett Trailer Corporation built it.

A great deal of work is concealed by the panelling on a van body, and in the past the variable nature of timber made bodybuilding a time-consuming business. Once standard metal components became generally available greater overall efficiency replaced much of the craftsmanship and it became possible for makers to produce kits of parts, like the body frame on this Commer of the mid-1950s, for unskilled labour to assemble.

ing, made a structure that was both stiff and durable. Large-sided pantechnicons have similar characteristics and their builders also tended to use sheet metal from an early period; even so, many van users preferred timber, sometimes using match boarding placed diagonally to gain rigidity.

To all intents and purposes only two structural metals are available to the bodybuilder – steel and aluminium. Economically their advantages are fairly balanced: a low initial price for steel is offset by the higher reclaim value of scrap aluminium, while the greater resistance to knocks possessed by steel is compensated for by the ease with which aluminium can be persuaded to adopt complicated shapes. Very often, the choice is determined by temporary supply shortages of one and the ready availability of the other but the greater ease with which steel can be satisfactorily welded and otherwise jointed has made it, over the years, the more popular material for many kinds of motor bodywork. This is not to imply that aluminium (more usually the lightweight alloys derived from it) has been ignored: one certain way of getting more payload onto a lorry without exceeding the legal limitations on gross weight is to reduce its unladen weight and, properly used, the light metals and their alloys can be useful in any campaign to 'add lightness' – a carefully designed light alloy body may easily weigh a third less than an equivalent wooden structure. An added attraction is the way in which the harder aluminium alloys can resist abrasion and shock loadings, all without the need for painting or other protection against weather and corrosion.

If a separate chassis frame is the most effective foundation on which to assemble running gear, a framed structure with separate cladding panels is

certainly a very convenient way to build up the bodywork. Unfortunately, making the traditional form of wooden framing is labour-intensive – and in most countries skilled labour of any kind is in short supply – as well as being very time-consuming. This combination of circumstances has condemned many old-established handicraft industries and it has very nearly killed this one. In its place have come systems of jig-building, which obviate much of the need for individual skill while at the same time making it a great deal easier to produce fleets of vehicles in which component parts are interchangeable, so reducing the variety of spare parts that have to be kept in stock and making it simpler to fit them.

Several manufacturers have applied these jig-built semi-automated methods to timber structures with a fair degree of success, but wood is too variable a material, and as vehicle sizes and capacities increased so did the amount of essential metal reinforcing, which added further to unproductive weight and complication. In many parts of the world, termites and other timber-consuming pests add yet another drawback to the use of wood.

As soon as sufficient demand existed, the light alloy manufacturers began to market metal sections suitable for almost every body-building purpose. These sections are made by extruding molten metal through shaped holes in dies, and an enormous variety is available, from simple angle and tee forms of the kind sold in handicraft shops, to extraordinarily complicated sections for special purposes. Light alloy extrusions have very largely replaced timber in many applications, and even extruded 'planks' are marketed for use in body sides and floors.

Inevitably, attempts have been made, with considerable success, to combine the functions of frame and panel. In a trend that began in America, light alloy or stainless steel sheet (neither need be painted, further reducing build times and weight) is pressed into corrugated patterns that make the thin metal very rigid indeed. When the ribbing runs horizontally some vertical framing is still required but the exterior of the completed body is easy to clean; vertical corrugations may need a horizontal stiffener or two, but the roof and floor do most of the work. Even timber – of a kind – can be used for self-supporting panelwork. In recent years a technique has been developed for coating both sides of a high quality plywood sheet with a thin layer of tough reinforced plastic; the result, perhaps 26 mm thick, can be obtained in sheets big enough to form a van side 12 m by 2·5 m in one piece, and needing no more support than that provided by roof, floor and ends. The resulting body is certainly easy to clean, withstands casual damage very well, and appears to be tolerably easy to repair.

Plastics, usually reinforced, are making slow if steady progress into goods vehicle body building, partly because the ability of these materials to assume an infinite variety of complicated shapes is not in much demand for lorries. Even so, van roofs are commonly made in translucent plastics, and sporadic attempts to use these materials in tanker construction may soon bear fruit.

Tanks, of course, are self-supporting and need no framing, providing they are more or less of

circular shape; indeed, when mounted on a chassis their inherent stiffness is generally greater than that of the lorry frame, which leads to problems in providing sufficiently flexible mountings. Tanks are also light in relation to the weight they can carry – and it soon began to be appreciated that the great strength of a tubular tank could perhaps supplant the vehicle chassis. Some tentative experiments have taken place, but so far no one has met any degree of commercial success building truly chassisless heavy lorries of any kind, although a considerable number of buses have no chassis. Yet very few semi-trailer tanks built in recent years have had conventional underframes, which at least underlines the validity of the idea, and as the number of independent vehicle makers continues to dwindle, together with the variety of designs that are marketed, longer production runs may well encourage further exploitation of the chassisless principle.

Another class of bodywork of considerable economic importance is the tipper, which in one guise or another has come to combine the characteristics of flat-bed, van and tanker. For a very long time – indeed, until mechanical loading became almost universal – tippers were virtually flats with detachable sides. It was essential that the sides hinged down so that labourers could shovel loads on board. With a hinged tailgate for discharging, it does not take much imagination to picture the resulting frailty of the body, particularly for such arduous work as rubble removal, in the days when

One of the very few attempts in recent times to break away from stereotyped thinking on commercial vehicle design was the Thompson tanker of 1968. It had a rear mounted engine, and much use was made of the inherent stiffness in a long tank to replace a conventional chassis. A very low line resulted: so low that cab doors in the usual places were impracticable.

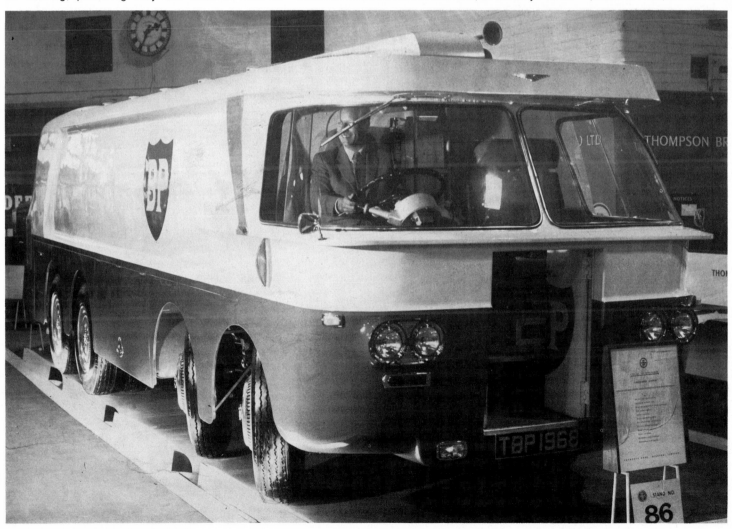

timber was the universal body material. Many tippers relied on a length of chain across the load to anchor the sides upright, a thoroughly unsatisfactory expedient.

Smaller-sized tipping lorries have always been in demand, however, and since there is rarely much call for novelty in their design, standard structures welded up from steel sheet with simple frame members in folded steel came to dominate the market. Corrosion is a hazard, but steel is easily welded and patched and on typically rough work – demolition or quarrying – the vehicles tend to wear out before rust becomes a problem. Designs have much improved in detail over the years, and clever use of press work produces tipper bodies that are stiff, robust, and which discharge their loads cleanly: internal corners are radiussed and smooth; and welding, which is used extensively, is calculated to obviate the stress-induced cracking that was once common.

When present-day maximum-length vehicles began to come into use, design and practice took another step forward with articulated semi-trailer tippers capable of holding 30 cu m or more. These impressive vehicles are considerable tributes to the designer's skill: light alloy plate and extrusions are usually the main materials adopted in their construction.

All these basic types of goods-carrying bodywork are suitable for general traffic, but increasing specialisation has inevitably given rise to whole families of vehicles precisely matched to their functions. Loading and unloading are, naturally enough, matters of great interest to most users and many lorries are designed almost entirely around these two factors. Even the simple flat can become specialised in this way: brickmakers, for example, commonly use essentially ordinary flat bodywork, fitted with a kind of travelling bridge crane; using this, one man can load and unload 20 tonnes or so of palleted bricks in minutes.

The widespread use of pallets – those small wooden platforms that make it possible for fork-lift trucks to handle so many cargoes – has led to a kind of half-platform, half-van body: a clear floor covered by a roof supported only by front and rear ends and removable struts. Fork trucks have access to the full length of both sides; weather protection is provided by curtains made from tough plastics-based material.

Another flat-bed speciality is the familiar lowloader, usually a semi-trailer in which the platform is kept as close to the ground as possible, keeping the overall height of awkward loads to a minimum and making loading and unloading easier. For many years it was almost a tradition for the wheels to be removable, leaving only a shallow ramp to be negotiated by the cargo. In more recent times, however, advances in hydraulics technology have made it possible to build trailers in which the front cranked swan-neck can be uncoupled and drawn clear with very little human effort, so that loading can take place from the front, leaving undisturbed the wheels, suspension and brake rigging. A

Skiploaders exemplify the way in which modern operators are often willing to add considerably to unladen weight, and thereby reduce payload, in the interests of quicker and easier cargo handling. These twin-boom machines can pick up, drop, or empty a skip in seconds: they can also load and transport small machinery, old cars and similar items.

modern curiosity among flat-bed semi-trailers is, strictly speaking, unable to carry a load by itself: the skeletal, as the name implies, is nothing more than a frame. It is, however, perfectly adapted to carry international-standard (International Standards Organisation) containers – special quick-release locking devices at the corners secure these big boxes firmly enough for the complete vehicle to behave as a single structure. Not all international containers are boxes, either: many tanks are cradled in strong frames which conform to the ISO box dimensions, and other body styles are available too.

Several humbler types of container have evolved during the last 40 years for refuse and rubbish disposal. Most easily recognised is the skip loader, where a distinctively shaped bin is lifted on and off by a pair of hydraulically powered arms on the transporting lorry. With hardly any adaptation, the same vehicle can self-load things like derelict cars, small road rollers and portable compressors. Not surprisingly, skip loaders, for the development of which American and German engineers must share the credit, are now in wide use. Less common is a modification of the same idea, but with its structural geometry arranged to lift larger bins and greater weights. Often the bins can be completely sealed, and this system is well adapted to accumulating and transporting noxious waste.

Less spectacular than these self-loading systems are modern versions of a very old idea indeed: a conventional-looking flat, sided or tipper body that runs on rails along the lorry chassis. When it has run far enough, it overbalances to tip its load or form a loading ramp. The body can also be run off altogether and lie on the ground. Manoeuvres are controlled by winch and chain or hydraulic ram, and the whole system combines a remarkable assembly of the functions of less versatile vehicles. It does not take much imagination to appreciate that all these detachable containers

are subject to a great deal of abuse and ill-treatment, and that they must therefore be very strongly built to achieve a reasonable service life. Operators are willing to accept the resultant weight penalty – which is significant – despite cargoes that are almost invariably low in value, or even worthless.

One of the most attractive aspects of articulation for many users is the ease with which one high-cost motive power unit can keep several low-cost semi-trailers fully employed, usually by having them loaded and unloaded while the tractor is in transit, occasionally by keeping trailers adapted for special purposes and coupling up only when required. If, however, the still weighty and maintenance-prone running gear under the trailers can be dispensed with, then so much the better. Lorry chassis fitted with lift-off bodywork provide one alternative, but their use implies cumbersome and expensive crane equipment, and they are thus not particularly suitable for replacing readily coupled and uncoupled artics, particularly for delivery work.

In the last 20 years or so, this has led to a whole range of self-supporting demountable body systems, another idea with its roots in the immediate post-First World War years. Once installed on its chassis, it takes a practised eye to recognise the demountable; yet when the time comes to exchange bodies it takes very few minutes to unfurl its legs and jack the body sufficiently clear for the chassis to be driven away. Remounting simply involves backing a chassis under the demountable and retracting its legs. A small hand-operated hydraulic power pack is often used to provide the jacking effort; an even neater solution is provided by two or three makers who modify carrying chassis by substituting an air suspension system at the rear. This can be deflated sufficiently to lower the vehicle and let it drive clear. An apparent hazard with any demountable is the vulnerability of the slender supporting legs to attack by carelessly

The advantages of being able to load one body, and unload another, while a third is actually in transit are apparent – indeed, such flexibility was deemed a great advantage of articulated trailers for urban deliveries. Many users now dispense with the semi-trailer and its running gear by using demountable bodies of this kind. Some incorporate jacks to lift the body; some, like this Hanomag Henschel, have air suspension that can be deflated to provide the necessary clearance.

driven vehicles, but this appears not to be a serious or even significant problem.

The ISO containers, decorated with labels from Tokyo, Moscow, New York and dozens of other far-away places, were essentially developed to meet the needs of constantly increasing international trade. Aimed at the same kind of traffic are the TIR (Transportes Internationale Routier) semi-trailers and drawbar trailers, common in Europe and on international routes served by European hauliers. Other vehicle types, usually vans of one kind or another, do run under TIR rules, but the distinctive full-size platform units, with low removable sides and a superstructure frame easily dismantled to load them with any kind of cargo within their capacity, were developed specifically for the work. Their frameworks are covered by tailored fabric sheets secured so that if properly assembled and sealed, national customs departments are

prepared to allow them across frontiers without inspecting and checking the loads. Elaborate regulations concerning sealing procedures at the points of departure, and such matters as accident repair, have to be closely followed by all operators of TIR vehicles.

The most significant types of van are the insulated and refrigerated specimens used to transport food and other temperature-sensitive cargoes. Before the days of plastics these normally resembled ordinary frame vans lined with thick slabs of cork and with inner skins of sheet metal and wood. Inevitably, joints leaked and the cork became saturated, seriously reducing the efficiency of the whole vehicle. Panelling is still favoured by some makers, although the modern insulant is made either from thick sheets of foamed plastic, or from foam plastic compounds pumped into the cavity between the inner and outer panelling. Either

It is not often that the purpose-made TIR semi-trailers are seen without their carefully tailored canvas covers in place. The slats and framing can be removed, and the sides lowered, to ease the tasks of loading and unloading, and the myriad little hooks along the sides and ends receive the elaborately laced securing ropes that are part of the international TIR customs convention. Barrieros built the tractor.

method results in a structure impervious to moisture and very rigid, but pride of place perhaps goes to the handful of manufacturers who make the entire body, including roof and floor, of glass reinforced plastics laminates, with integral foamed insulant. This provides an apparently unbeatable standard of hygiene.

Used intelligently, simple insulated bodies are perfectly satisfactory for many duties – making local deliveries from factory or cold store to shops, for example – but they cannot be expected to hold temperatures at a low level for days on end or, of course, actively to reduce temperatures. That is a task for the 'fridge' vans, which have their own refrigerator units, usually mounted high on the front bulkhead of the van or, more rarely, under the floor of a semi-trailer. Usually the unit has its own engine, which often seems to add more to traffic noise than the lorry itself; electrically-powered

ones have the advantage that they can be plugged into an external power supply during overnight stops or on board ship during sea crossings.

The road tanker, an apparently simple and straightforward way of transporting large quantities of liquids, has rarely been either simple or straightforward. For one thing, as soon as capacities began to exceed about 2,500 litres, it became necessary to divide tanks into compartments and incorporate baffles in order to prevent part-loads from surging and upsetting vehicle stability on the road. Then, while many loads like wine, petrol or milk can be relied upon to pour themselves into or out of a tanker, some fluids require the assistance of a pump at collection or delivery points; fortunately it is a simple matter to take the drive for a pump from the vehicle gearbox. Some cargoes require assistance of another kind: substances like tar, sulphur, fats and chocolate must be heated

A heavily insulated body is often sufficient to maintain ex-cold-store cargoes – for example, over short journeys or local delivery schedules. Longer distances, however, demand the greater complication of a refrigerator unit mounted on the vehicle. It must be separately powered to allow for periods when the lorry engine is not running. This semi-trailer has its refrigerator mounted on the front bulkhead.

A complication inside many tankers that is unsuspected by most passers-by is the system of bulkheads or baffles that serve to brace the whole assembly while, at the same time, dividing it into separate compartments. These make it possible to carry several different sorts of cargo in one vehicle and minimise the tendency to dangerous surging as the vehicle brakes or negotiates corners.

before their consistency is thin enough to pump. For regular journeys of known duration it is often possible to rely on insulation to keep a load liquid; otherwise a steam supply at the delivery point must be connected to a heating coil within the tank.

In recent years another development has taken tankers into solids transport. Provided they can be mixed sufficiently thoroughly with air, many powders take on some of the characteristics of a liquid and may be blown or pumped through piping. Cement, sugar, flour and semi-manufactured plastics are among the materials regularly transported and discharged in this way, and the process is often helped by arranging the tank body to tip.

Blurred distinctions between tankers and tippers, liquid and solid cargoes, are echoed by a tribe of lorries which combine some characteristics from vans, tankers and tippers. Grains and animal feedstuffs must be handled gently if they are not to crumble and degrade; they are light and bulky, and are produced and consumed in large quantities.

The standard vehicle evolved to meet these requirements is a high-sided tipper with a roof of either metal or tarpaulin. It is loaded by folding back the roof and allowing the cargo to flow in. To discharge, a rotary valve under the floor at the rear is set in motion – the valve comprises large pockets which pick up the granular material without breaking it – while the body is tipped just enough to give a clean discharge. Sometimes the sides can be folded down flat for carrying bagged loads when bulk loads are not available.

In one sense, coal and other solid fuels are similar to cattle cake and pig nuts – they are easily crumbled and degraded, with the additional complication that many customers want only small quantities. One successful solution comprises an open body which in cross-section resembles the letter V. At the bottom of the V an endless belt forms a moving floor, so that by starting and stopping the belt precise quantities can be discharged – usually straight into a bag standing on a vehicle-mounted weighing machine. An adaptation of this design, with the final discharge down a chute that can be swung from side to side, has been used successfully for backfilling trenches and for placing concrete.

Concrete is a difficult material to transport, for it is heavy, abrasive, and chemically unstable; no one wants a load of concrete more than half an hour after the water has been added, least of all the owner, whose truck-mounted mixer it will ruin. Yet a great deal of time, space and material on building sites can be saved if concrete is dispensed from a central batching plant, with the equally useful advantage that this will make it easier to maintain product specification. What is more, with careful planning, it may be possible to arrange bulk material deliveries by rail or water to the batcher. Getting the mixed concrete to site can then be timed to meet requirements exactly, and the

Bagged deliveries are expensive, and worthwhile savings can be made when powdered or granular commodities are transported in bulk. Farm feedstocks are among the cargoes which, in addition, readily degrade through too much or careless handling, and a satisfactory alternative to the traditional sack is this kind of tipper. A special rotary valve at the rear discharges the load gently and evenly, while air pressure blows it into storage silos.

composition and consistency can be prearranged by telephone. Each load is thoroughly mixed during the delivery journey, and water is added from tanks on the lorry just before unloading. Opinions differ over whether to derive the power to turn the mixer drum from the vehicle engine or from a separate power unit carried on the chassis; but the latter can be frame-mounted with the drum, and the whole mixer assembly removed as one for maintenance or installation on another chassis.

Auxiliary power units for mixers are only one example of machinery added to help the bodywork of a lorry perform its functions. The most useful are the tipping gears; in horse-drawn days most tipping wagons were two-wheeled, and the point of balance was such that, when empty they rested normally and when loaded they tended to tip – a simple locking pin, easily withdrawn, kept the whole thing stable. Not many motor builders could economically provide such simple convenience.

For the first three or four decades of motor transport a great many tipper bodies were raised by hand, seemingly endless turning of a crank just behind the cab causing a long vertical screw at the

Transit concrete mixer design has changed somewhat over the last half-century. The earlier version *(above)* has a cylindrical chamber with spiral mixer bars, and water is carried in the longitudinal top tanks – which cannot have helped stability. Most modern machines *(left)* have the double cone revolving drum, an arrangement which keeps the centre of gravity acceptably low.

front to lift the body slowly. But efforts were soon made to mechanise this chore and steam builders again took the lead, using the great reserves of power at their disposal and the ease with which it could be harnessed. At first, water was the medium used for the literally hydraulic gear on tippers; by the 1920s, more convenient oil was being used and the gears were more readily identifiable with modern ideas – simple piston and cylinder assemblies that took their power from pumps driven from the vehicle gearboxes.

These power take-offs have become the time-honoured way of driving ancillary equipment of all kinds, although internal limitations mean that it is rarely possible to use more than a portion of the full engine capacity. Tipping gears divide, broadly, into two types: a long multi-stage ram (sometimes paired) standing at the extreme front of the body, and a much shorter ram housed under the body. Advantages are claimed for both. Front rams certainly have a mechanical advantage in that they pick up the load at one end, and there is no need to add any local reinforcement to the body, which, if it is stiff enough to carry its load, should be able to

withstand lifing from one end. When long bodies are fully extended, they are probably also more stable with full height support. On the other hand, underbody gears are completely protected against accidental damage, although they do demand considerable extra stiffening of the floor framing, particularly in the area where the tipping ram brings its lifting effort to bear. However, in those countries where tipping drawbar trailers are in common use, the ability to also tip sideways is essential, and that is only feasible with underbody gear.

A singularly useful device that had to wait to benefit from technical developments elsewhere is the lorry-mounted crane. Isolated examples were made during the 1920s and even earlier, when an American company marketed a lorry crane driven by a power take-off from the gearbox – then a very advanced concept – but these early efforts had much of the riveter's art and a lot of chain about them; although some operators found them useful, both performance and range were limited. With the advent of cheap and reliable hydraulics equipment after 1950, all that changed: neat little cranes are now included in the specification of many lorries, and by touching a small lever one man can effortlessly load or unload cargo weighing a tonne or more, and place it precisely where it is wanted. Most operate simply as cranes, but with detachable accessories they can become fork trucks lifting laden pallets, or small grab excavators able to take the labour out of loading rubble and other debris into high-sided tippers.

Winches have been standard equipment in some kinds of road transport from the very beginning; strategically placed on the chassis, a good winch is not only useful for pulling suitable loads on to the vehicle (perhaps in collaboration with a simple davit), but also for recovering the truck itself if it runs into soft ground. Many a laden lorry and trailer, faced with the problem of moving across a field – or even an icy slope – has done so by running out its winch rope, anchoring itself to a conveniently placed tree, and pulling. No low-loader is complete without a winch, either: many units are hand-powered even now, but the ever-useful gearbox power take-off driving a small hydraulic motor on the winch is common; now that vehicle batteries can be recharged rapidly while in service, electrically powered units are also available.

Another invaluable electrically powered adjunct to the modern goods-carrying vehicle is the tailhoist, a platform that doubles as tailboard and elevator. Out of use, it is hinged up to act as part of the body; while loading or unloading it drops to form a small horizontal platform that can rise and fall from body floor to road surface. More refined versions rise higher still, to ease the task of double-stacking loads. The tailhoist is really just an updated version of another helpful scheme that originated before the First World War. Body platform heights were almost universally high (and it is worth recalling that the average stature of men was measurably less than it is now) and one ingenious firm arranged the mountings of its tailboards so that the boards hinged down to form a full-width rigid step approximately half-way between floor and road – an idea of the past that seems worth reviving.

Considering that the lorry cab forms a working place for one or two men, and that it may well be inhabited for a total of 20 hours a day, very few manufacturers or owners can be accused of having devoted much time or trouble to improving its comfort or convenience. For the first 20 years of motor transport, even protection against the weather was rudimentary and often absent altogether; for the next 40 years cabs were uncomfortable and noisy; only since about 1960 has adequate attention been paid to improving the daily lot of the lorry driver.

Constructional methods and materials have generally kept much in step with those used for large passenger cars, and for many years wooden framings clad in simple sheet metal panels were used for most vehicles. Many chassis manufacturers have traditionally kept their direct interests in body building at a low level (although they have always reserved the right to approve superstructures destined for their products). Many had more or less formal joint marketing arrangements with individual bodybuilders, which led to a general similarity of appearance between the products mounted

Without vehicle-mounted lifts expensive loading docks are needed wherever a lorry is to pick up a load that is too heavy to manhandle, and where no crane or fork truck is available. A particularly pleasing application for tail-hoists makes it possible to lift into welfare vehicles those condemned to life in wheelchairs.

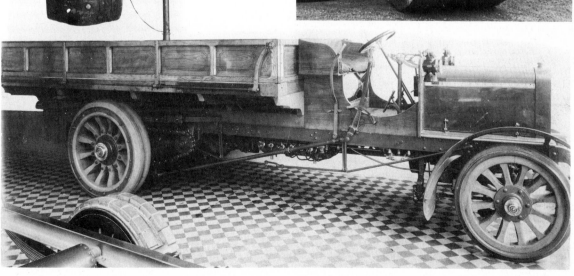

A simple manually-operated jib crane would clearly be a great help in loading casks onto this early Commer (left). Observe the beautiful workmanship put into the varnished timber body – and also the truss rods that brace the simple rolled steel channel chassis. A particularly useful modern-day fitting is the hydraulic crane (left, above). Most are used simply as cranes, to lift loads on and off, but with small adaptation they can be made to pick up rubbish and excavated material, so that one man, the driver, can load and transport without assistance.

The cab has yet to be built on this Albion of the 1940s, but it will clearly be a difficult business to do much to make life comfortable for the crew. The engine bonnet is made of sheet metal with no attempt to incorporate silencing material, and all the controls are rigidly mounted to the chassis, and will thus transmit a great deal of noise and vibration.

For the volume producers—in this case General Motors subsidiary Bedford—pressed steel cabs offering reasonable comfort were economically possible.

on their chassis, particularly where the cabs were concerned. Notable exceptions to this practice were those companies, mainly American and their imitators, which from 1930 onwards began to mass-produce medium-weight goods chassis. They soon found that the amount of labour and time demanded by coachbuilt cabs, even using assembly-line techniques, was quite out of proportion to the rapidity and ease with which the chassis could be assembled. Since most of these companies also built passenger cars, it was no great step for them to adapt the pressed-steel techniques then coming into use for cars to the production of large cabs.

Cabs were therefore either coachbuilt or pressed steel until the 1950s, when several companies turned to the newly developed laminated reinforced plastics in the hope that these infinitely adaptable materials would make it possible to produce economically in small quantities cabs as stylish in appearance as the car-inspired mass-producers were then making in pressed steel. From the appearance point of view plastics were very successful—almost too successful, for some designers allowed enthusiasm to oust good taste!—but even the most exuberantly styled cab was completely corrosion and rot proof, while accidental damage could be easily repaired; it seemed that this form of construction had a bright future. Until, that is, the modern era of statutory crash-testing for road vehicles, when it was found to be no easy matter to build a plastics cab capable of withstanding the onerous treatment received in testing laboratories. In addition, by the end of the 1960s, the number of lorries in use was rising so rapidly that even the small-volume chassis builders were making too many vehicles for plastics cabs to be economically attractive: laminate construction, like coachbuilding, is a labour-intensive activity.

Thus there was a marked revival of interest in steel structures just at the time when cab comfort became a major selling point, and those manufacturers unable to justify the expense of making their own cabs had to turn to specialist sub-contractors, who have become adept at camouflaging a handful of standard pressings to suit the desires of competing customers, or even to buying cabs from rival chassis makers. It now costs very nearly as much to tool up a factory to produce a modern lorry cab as it does to make a whole passenger car, and hard economics have produced some strange bedfellows, particularly in Europe. Worse: the absence of a suitable cab at a suitable price has caused the demise of old and honoured firms.

In the days when engines needed frequent and often major attention, most commercial vehicles had their power units conventionally mounted under a front bonnet, where there was plenty of room and it was generally easy to get complete access to everything. It was a different matter when the cab moved forward to cover the engine, and many of the earliest cab-overs were lofty indeed, to retain good accessibility to both sides of the power unit. A little later one or two firms arranged matters so that the whole cab could be lifted bodily off the chassis, which gave an access unrivalled until tilt-cabs came into general use during the 1950s and 1960s, although American makers were experimenting with tilt-cabs before the Second World War. Now tilt-cabs are almost universal on medium-weight and heavier trucks, because modern engines and their ancillary equipment are so complicated and tightly packed into the limited available space that it would hardly be feasible to service and maintain them through the handholes and hatches that once served well enough.

In most applications, the fact that the cab is occasionally required to hinge forward almost clear of the chassis matters not at all, but the introduction of the tilt-cab caused some dismay among bodybuilders and users who favoured the type of van known in Britain as the Luton—the kind which has an extension to the body forward over the cab roof. This renewed difficulty of engine access was probably a factor in the growing demand for vans in which the cab is an integral part of the body. This makes it very easy to incorporate extra seating for the large crews needed for work such as furniture removal, while there is also enough room inside to cope with most engine work. Some users now forsake lorry chassis altogether when ordering a new maximum capacity van and instead select an underfloor-engined bus chassis. With a virtually flat frame from front to back, on a machine intended to carry all-enveloping bodywork and to be serviced from outside, the attractions are real.

Even so, although makers are prepared to supply bare chassis, or chassis incorporating just a front scuttle and windscreen, most modern users clearly prefer to take a fully fitted standard cab. It is not easy to equal the levels of interior trim and comfort provided in these straight-from-the-catalogue units.

When something is as conspicuous and expensive as a lorry most owners naturally regard its paintwork as something of importance, if only because of the time and cost involved. Even today, when self-protecting materials like plastics and aluminium alloys are in wide use, most owners still paint them in a spirit of pride or to maintain a corporate identity. In the days when wood and canvas were universally used, painting was a serious and vital matter, and since skilled labour came cheaply a great many commercial vehicles enjoyed the sort of loving care and multi-coated paintwork that was commonly applied to the better sorts of passenger car. Most went further, for there are few finer potential billboards than the side panels of a lorry, and signwriters seized these splendid opportunities to indulge themselves in beautifully lettered, gold leafed, backshaded renditions of company names and products.

The fine-lettering tradition lingered almost to the present day, but background paintwork increasingly reflected a growing preoccupation with profit margins and vehicle utilisation. Every advance in the paintmakers' alchemy was seized upon, and a lorry can now be liveried in a day or two, its owner's trademark displayed large – but applied in a few minutes, as a pre-printed layer of adhesive plastic film.

Above: A combination that looks strange in Britain, home of the chassis, and strange in West Germany, home of the cab. Atkinson, during the late 1960s badly in need of a better cab, turned to Krupp; but the partnership failed to endure. Both makers have since gone, too.

Sometimes lorry users turn to bus chassis, usually as the basis for maximum capacity vans. An Australian firm used a Leyland underfloor engined bus for this most unusual car transporter, in which not a scrap of available length is wasted.

97

Unladen weight versus payload, the sum total to be kept within the law – that is the perennial problem of most hauliers. Sometimes, when tipper operating conditions ar good, albeit not on public roads, largely standard chassis, like this Mercedes, can ignore normal precepts and be fitted with special heavy duty bodywork for arduous loads. The cab roof protector indicates that loading machinery drivers are sometimes careless.

LOST CAUSES

Viewed with hindsight, the path of commercial vehicle development has been remarkably straight and consistent: look at any present-day lorry – or bus, for that matter – and it clearly cannot be denied by its forebears. Nearly all the aspects in which earlier generations differ from their successors are mere details, intended to overcome contemporary difficulties caused by methods and materials and, in their turn, superseded by time and events. But there have also been a few *culs-des-sac* along the way; lines of thought which for one reason or another failed to justify the hopes, effort, time and money lavished on them by fond protagonists.

Pride of place in this melancholy band of lost causes must go to steam traction in both its road-going forms: as separate locomotive tractors and as load-carrying wagons. The first was clearly blood-brother to the agricultural steam engine, and hardly anyone outside Britain seriously attempted to use such locomotives for road haulage. Even in Britain, the home of steam power in every form, restrictions on weight, dimensions and speed limited the use of large machines to specialised heavy and slow haulage applications; in this field steam was still used well into the 1930s and 1940s, long after internal combustion had shown its ability to haul or carry single loads of 100 tonnes. These great steamers, weighing 15 tonnes or more, 7 m long, and with hind wheels 2 m diameter, formed a

grand spectacle, both in workaday haulage form – slowly but effortlessly heading a many-wheeled low trailer carrying a giant transformer or boiler – or as a richly caparisoned showman's locomotive. For the first 30 years, travelling circus and pleasure fairground proprietors relied heavily on steam for both traction and generating electric power. These gentlemen, with an astute nose for business, and aware of the eye-catching propensities of their steeds, spent small fortunes on intricate decorations and paintwork, in which quantities of highly polished brass were considered essential. Happily, although they have now been entirely supplanted by diesel power, a few of these giants from an earlier age still survive to remind the world of long-forgotten but once-famous makers – Burrell, Fowler, Garrett and others – and their occasional public appearances never fail to demonstrate that what the present-day generation of showgrounds have gained in efficiency they have certainly lost in glamour.

At the other extreme of steam locomotion, both in size and excitement, lay the little tractors, a peculiarly British breed that came about in response to the Motor Car Act of 1903, one of the earliest pieces of legislation anywhere to recognise the new motoring age and which, more specifically, encouraged the use of haulage machines weighing in the region of 5 tonnes. That was not much for

Steam, needing no complicated or fragile transmission, and capable of exerting a smooth and steady effort, is in many ways ideal for heavy haulage. It is also a great deal more picturesque than the internal combustion traction that has taken its place.

steam power, which was usually heavy, and steam tractors tended to be used as replacements for heavy horses, even hauling what were once horse vehicles.

All these traction machines were effectively overtaken by events: increasing vehicle speeds and density showed them to be slow and cumbersome in traffic, and as other modes of transport improved, it became first possible and then sensible to abandon steam.

The same arguments should not, and in some respects did not, apply to steam wagons. Load carrying steamers waxed during the first decade of the century and waned during the second; with very few exceptions they were again a British preoccupation. In the early years a few makers in mainland Europe also tried, including two French companies who looked to British designs (Brulé working to Thornycroft ideas while Malevez used Lifu

patents). Perhaps the most commercially successful of the non-British Europeans was the French Exshaw, which lasted into the 1920s. In America a myriad of firms – Stanley, White, Baker, Coulthard and others – made a handful of vehicles; most were lightweight vans, although Halsey produced an 8-tonner and Coulthard built a heavy wagon nearly identical to the undertypes sold under the same name in Britain.

Steam could have been successful in the field of freight transport and the last examples, including Henschels built in Germany during the first year or two of the Second World War, years after almost everyone else had given up, showed that steam was perfectly capable of meeting diesel or petrol engined contemporaries on level terms – and of beating them hands down. Yet such successes do no more than obscure the fact that steam wagons were never very significant numerically; as the years went by, internal-combustion engined competitors pushed them steadily along the payload-carrying scale until they finally disappeared.

Why was something so apparently suitable as steam – well established, requiring no complicated transmission, capable of handling great weights and reliable – so rapidly overcome by demonstrably

inferior rivals? No single answer is either satisfactory or accurate, for the demise of steam came about from the interaction of several factors. One was certainly too many manufacturers in too small an overall market, with the result that none were able to earn enough to indulge in the expensive business of product development. Almost all of them began life as agricultural blacksmiths, a calling which is expected to provide goods of great strength and reliability; old habits died hard, with the result that most steam wagons appeared to offer ludicrous tare-to-payload ratios. In fact, their ability to absorb huge overloads made such reckonings academic – unfortunately, the resulting gross weights then attracted the enmity of road maintenance authorities. The great durability of these traditionally built wagons was something else that militated against steam: what is often regarded as anti-steam legislation during the 1930s was, in fact, intended to do no more than recognise the contemporary state of road transport with revised construction and use regulations. It was merely unfortunate that the steam interest was so small and that so many existing steam vehicles were incapable of operating economically within the new and generally desirable scheme of things. Another

Above: Circus and pleasure fairground proprietors seized upon steam power not only to haul their trains of wagons from one site to another, but also for generating electricity – the generator of this preserved Fowler is in the usual position, on a bracket right at the front. Showmen needed no lessons in attracting audiences, and vied with each other in the quality and exuberance of decoration applied to their steamers.

Left: A notable vehicle in several respects: a Bordeaux-built Purrey-Exshaw steam wagon of about 1914, and therefore one of the few commercially successful steamers not emanating from Britain. It was also a 6 tonner, a high capacity for its time, and the hydraulically operated tipping gear shows one disadvantage of side discharge: it drops the cargo around and under the wheels.

Work that undoubtedly
belongs to road transport is
the fetching and carrying of
the vast quantities of
materials needed for any
modern civil engineering
project: rarely indeed can
rail or water even begin to
compete. The fleet of MAN
trucks *(above)* make the
point that when the
expense, weight, and extra
complication can be
justified, more or less
standard chassis can be
adapted to four-wheel drive.
The Magirus Deutz *(right)* is
typical of eight-wheeled
tippers produced by several
rival factories. The AEC 6 by
4 *(far right)* shows that good
traction and normal on-road
characteristics can be
achieved by standard
chassis which have not
undergone expensive
modifications.

FUEL COST FOR GARRETT WAGON
3 TON ½ᴰ PER MILE

Park Bridge Iron Works

WORLD'S RECORD for FUEL & WATER CONSUMPTION.

Above: A picture that shows more clearly than words why the overtype steam wagon could be no more than a *cul de sac* on the road of vehicle development. The Garrett is rated at 3 tonnes – although it would certainly be able to take much more than that – and something like half its overall length is occupied by the boiler and machinery. Observe, too, the crewman, sitting half in and half out of the cab, and the very poor forward visibility. But overtypes were tough, and cheap to run.

Although a few steamers were made in later years, it may fairly be claimed that the last production wagons for general sale were Sentinels of the late 1930s. Given a sympathetic driver these machines were quite capable of outperforming contemporary diesel or petrol engined lorries, something a handful of survivors were still demonstrating many years later. For this final apotheosis of steam the makers provided a largely automated boiler and firing system capable of being handled by one man: controls were generally similar to those in internal combustion vehicles.

interesting suggestion at the time was that traditionally-minded owners of steamers had geared their operations to these overweight machines, and

looked askance at proposals to market lightweight vehicles in a more modern idiom.

To all intents and purposes only one manufacturer, Sentinel, survived to build steam wagons on a commercial scale into the 1940s – and these, in their turn, underlined the last and perhaps most damning weakness of steam: that while it can be made as simple to drive as internal combustion, this can only be done at the expense of much greater mechanical complexity. Balancing the demands of road and load against boiler capacity and achieving an overall operating economy require either drivers of an uncommonly high calibre or automated control systems the like of which are quite unknown in any vehicle maintenance facility – then or now. In not-dissimilar circumstances Sir Henry Royce remarked that complicated mechanisms do not matter so long as they are reliable. It is a philosophy that few lorry owners would care to adopt.

In this environmentally-conscious age, incidentally, it is worth adding one small footnote: steam wagons were once preferred for night work in many British cities because they made so much less noise than petrol or diesel engined vehicles.

Steamers may be both complicated and commercially extinct, but neither can really be said of battery-electric traction. Yet it warrants inclusion as a cause that may be lost, if only because of its oft-promised but always deferred advance to bigger and better things. Indeed, so far as large capacity battery-electrics are concerned, their heyday was over by the mid-1930s. Whether they return in some oil-starved future remains to be seen.

The great snag with battery-electrics is the battery, and it is a remarkable fact that the perform-

ance characteristics of these vehicles have altered hardly at all during eight decades: about 80 km is still the maximum distance that can be covered on one charge. Of course, there have been improvements in vehicle performance to match contemporary traffic requirements, some worthwhile savings in battery weight and reductions in energy losses through the control systems; but during all these years, contemporary economic balances between energy storage capacity and payload have never allowed the battery-electric to stray far beyond that invisible but very real cordon.

The tangible if elusive advantages of stored electricity as a source of power for road vehicles are so great, however, that in certain severely restricted spheres – notably localised urban deliveries – considerable numbers of small battery-electrics are in use. For door-to-door deliveries, where speed is unimportant and the silent exhaust-free characteristics of the electric are particularly welcome, they survive. But even here, hard economics are pressing: fewer and fewer retail organisations can afford the ever-rising cost of the labour required for domestic deliveries, and as roundsmen join the list of forgotten things, there is a real danger that their quiet, self-effacing, reliable little battery-electric vans may do so too.

If they do, they will join the quite-extinct large capacity electric lorry. This was never common, for the twin curses of limited range and few charging points militated against it, but during the 1920s and 1930s two or three makers were offering capacities of 5 tonnes or more. General Vehicles in Britain made perhaps the largest – an articulated version of an existing 5 tonnes capacity lorry. This giant of its kind could take a payload of 10 tonnes and with

a useful speed of about 15 km/h was intended for general cartage. This was unusual: many big electrics were intended (or at any rate sold) for more humble duties such as refuse collection.

Articulation might have done something to mitigate some of the biggest drawbacks to battery traction, for the high unladen weight (typically, the mid-1920s French-built Crochat weighed 6 tonnes for its 5 tonnes payload, while a Berliet produced for some comparative trials of alternative fuels in 1923 weighed 6·6 tonnes for its 5 tonnes capacity) would have been spread over more revenue-earning cargo space, and the ease with which the motive power unit could be coupled and uncoupled should have reduced the problem of limited mileage between battery charges. But it was not to be, although one of the few sizeable fleets of articulated battery-electrics to last for any length of time survived until quite recent years in central London, where a number of 6 tonnes capacity machines crept silently around the night-time streets, performing sundry municipal duties with a minimum of disturbance to local residents.

Contemporary chemists persevere in their search for a combination of materials able at once to hold more energy, accept faster recharging, weigh much less and cost no more than lead-acid batteries. Hopes are being raised by lithium-sulphur and sodium-sulphur, which operate at uncomfortably high temperatures; and by zinc-chlorine, which demands a degree of refrigeration. The first is said to give three times the output of an equivalent lead-acid battery, but the proponents of these dramatic alternatives are inclined to answer evasively when closely questioned about the added risks in serious accidents.

This motor racing team shows its concern with overall operating efficiency by having an air deflector fitted on to the roof of the Mercedes tractor. These deflectors, seemingly crude in form and fixture, are capable of reducing to a marked degree the turbulence caused by pulling a flat-fronted box through the air at high speeds. Considerable improvements in fuel consumption can result.

Refuse collection is another task well matched to battery traction, for the low speed is no drawback and the silence a positive advantage. Many makers, after the angular days of the 1920s, contrived pleasantly curved styling for their products: the Electricar *(right)* is a typical example. Much of the durability and long life of the battery-electric came from its simplicity, and the mid-1940s Metrovick layout *(right, below)* shows how it was done. A steering column; two-pedal (controller left, brake right) control; direction reversing switch; handbrake. The speed controller drum lying above the front axle is revolved from the foot pedal. A single motor lies where the gearbox of a petrol vehicle would be.

If there is still some hope that battery-electrics will one day achieve the dazzling future so often predicted for them, it can safely be said that their nearest relatives, the trolley lorries, are quite dead. Indeed, so few were ever made and used that it might almost be said they never really lived. The trolley lorry was simple, and followed the theory which led to so many successful trolley bus systems – those useful hybrids of bus and tram – being installed throughout the world. Given a fixed route, sufficient demand and available electric power, why use something as complicated and undesirable as a noisy, fume-emitting, unreliable petrol vehicle? But while passenger-carrying routes can remain unchanged for years, a lorry which cannot stray more than a metre or two from a fixed path soon becomes a liability. Quietly (for silence was a great attribute) the handful of trolley lorries therefore faded away.

Somewhat less silently but probably just as completely (save for three or four surviving museum pieces) the petrol-electric has also departed for that nirvana of blighted hopes. It combined at once the smoothness and general desirability of electric traction with the operational flexibility inherent in a self-contained internal combustion engine; in theory, it should have had a long and moderately useful career. Unfortunately its separate and large generator and motor weighed a great deal more than the satisfactory and reliable clutches and gearboxes that became generally available from approximately 1927; at the same

Latter-day battery power is still hemmed in with the restrictions of old, but new and determined attempts are being made to minimise them. A promising line of development is being directed at adapting standard production bodyshells and running gear to electric traction: the Bedford CF van is one that needs acceptably limited modification on the assembly line to fit it for petrol, diesel, or electric power, this one having been converted to electric traction as part of an experiment by Lucas.

time, they cost much more to make from very much more expensive materials, and if there was ever a combination anathema to both makers and purchasers of commercial vehicles it is cost allied to weight.

Right at the end of the petrol-electric era, in the late 1920s, Faun in Germany chose to compound the weight problem by resurrecting another Lost Cause, the deceptively attractive idea of putting a separate hub-mounted electric motor into each drive wheel. Unfortunately, motors capable of exerting useful power at the comparatively low speeds achieved by vehicle road wheels must also be heavy; in the days when great weight was also a characteristic of live driving axles this might not have mattered so much and some early battery-electric lorries and trolley buses dispensed with the complexities of propeller shafts and differentials by using hub-mounted motors, although water and dirt must have been formidable hazards. Faun, a company traditionally concerned with making vehicles for special purposes, wanted to avoid the problems of fitting a conventional transmission into a transporter with a very low loading platform.

Several petrol-electrics demonstrated the versatility of their power trains by serving, with only small modification, as mobile arc welding plants in shipyards and other places where plenty of current could be usefully combined with the ability to carry a lot of ancillary equipment. And, long after the last of their kind for commercial use had left the assembly lines, hundreds of petrol-electrics were built by Tilling-Stevens (probably the most tenacious manufacturer engaged in this particular Lost Cause) for the British Army, which used them for years as the essential components of mobile searchlight units. Nor should it be forgotten that essentially similar transmissions are still used all over the world in diesel-electric railway locomotives, where providing an adequate all-mechanical means of getting power to the wheels is difficult.

When power units were heavy in relation to output, and mass transport of goods by road was unknown, it was inevitable that thoughts would turn to the use of locomotives hauling trains. All the familiar limitations on payload capacity imposed by road surfaces, tyres, braking and the rest could, it seemed, be overcome simply by using fleets of low-cost vehicles; since relatively few tractors would be required the high individual cost and the impossibility of mass-producing such machinery became irrelevant. Operationally, regular routes could be established with staging posts at which tractors might be exchanged for servicing, while the mix of vehicles in each train could be readily adjusted to suit demand: flat trucks, vans – even omnibuses. The whole would amount to a railway with none of the artificial restraints imposed by huge investments in track and other fixed assets.

Since they were capable of generating sizeable quantities of current while standing still, and with very little modification, it follows that petrol-electrics found their way into diverse applications. They made excellent bases for welding sets and searchlights, and this Tilling-Stevens of 1922 formed the mount for what may well have been the first lorry-mounted crane in the modern sense.

Many fine-grained materials can be treated almost as liquids when they are loaded and unloaded: flour, hauled by the Seddon Atkinson *(far left)*, is one of them. To speed the unloading process the tank semi-trailer tips, and to reduce unladen weight to a minimum a conventional trailer chassis and tipping gear are abandoned in favour of this ingenious arrangement.

Away from public roads some interesting things can be done by outwardly standard vehicles. The Leyland *(above)* used for aeroplane refuelling, carries something like twice the load that it would be permitted outside the airport gates. But level surfaces and low speeds form excellent operating conditions.

To most people milk, like wine, comes in bottles: the notion of it arriving in great road tankers is, at the least, strange. Yet if the product is to arrive fresh and cheap, fast bulk transport is essential. The pair of Fiats with trailers *(left)* are engaged in an Alpine run.

111

The earliest road trains, during the middle of the nineteenth century, were inevitably steam powered; the new generation, from 1900 on, were usually petrol engined. The German Freibahn was an exception, returning to steam and going to great trouble to obtain four-wheel drive on the tractor.

Modern road trains have no need of traction assistance from the trailers. This combination built during the mid-1960s to meet an Australian requirement, used a specially-built Scammell to haul 100 tonne consignements of iron ore.

All these considerations were clearly in the mind of the versatile young Lieutenant Crompton when, during the 1860s, he somehow persuaded the British Government to allow him to build two such road trains for India. These worked well enough, but convention and railways eventually won the day. When the road train appeared again it was essentially an internal combustion-engined affair, and one with a strong military tinge. Perhaps the first in the field was the French Renard, which used a large-engined tractor that transmitted its power through jointed propeller shafts to a pair of road wheels on each of several separate trailers, and which had steering arranged so that each trailer followed accurately in the wheeltracks of those in front. Renard demonstrated its ability to transport more than 15 tonnes at 15 km/h, an impressive performance for 1907. The British Daimler concern made the Renard under licence, but both military

and Empire authorities quickly saw that their transport needs might be met more effectively in other ways. This was a view not immediately shared in America, where the Alden-Sampson design adopted a much more elegant system for transmitting the drive: the tractor comprised a petrol-electric generator and electric motors were fitted to the wheels on the centre axle of six-wheeled trailers, thereby dispensing with wear-prone drive shafts. The French Crochat factory tried a very similar plan, as did Müller in Berlin, which used a tractor and six driven wagons to carry more than 30 tonnes at 13 km/h for the German army.

An earlier German design, the appropriately named Freibahn ('Freeway'), avoided what had become petrol-engined conventionality by using a steam tractor, while what was quite possibly the last step along this interesting dead-end in commercial vehicle development was the road train

built by AEC in England for use in Australia in 1933: the load-carrying diesel-engined tractor transmitted drive to the wheels of a pair of trailers, the whole offering a payload capacity of 15 tonnes. It worked well, on unmade roads and off them, and was credited by local residents with being the only thing to keep Northern Australia alive during the Second World War. But the AEC sowed the seeds of its own undoing: it was so successful that it generated enough traffic to justify building a proper road, suitable for much cheaper conventional production vehicles. So it is that here, as in many parts of the world, the road train lives on in the form of maximum size articulated lorries hauling one or two equally large drawbar trailers.

These modern tractors have only their rear wheels driven – indeed, not a few tandem-axle lorries, particularly from the Swedish manufacturers Volvo and Scania, manage very well indeed with only one axle of the pair driven, for modern design and materials can produce final drive units quite able to withstand the enormous loads imposed on them. For the first quarter of this century, however, there was a feeling that to drive all the wheels of a lorry or road tractor was, at the least, advisable. Vienna-based Gräf und Stift built a 4 by 4 for road work in 1908; the American Peerless was another, intended expressly for trailer work; and so was the four-wheel drive Walter which played a part in the early Goodyear pneumatic tyre experiments.

The nearest to success four-wheel drive came for on-road haulage was the large fleet of American FWD chassis left behind in Europe after the First World War. These performed well and spawned some descendants but even in the earliest days there was hardly ever any need for the complexities of all-wheel drive and as ordinary vehicles improved in reliability the need dwindled to vanishing point. Now there is really no on-road demand at all, and the thousands of four-wheel, six-wheel, and even eight-wheel drive lorries in service

Many Ford parts went into the Garner Straussler. Externally it looked conventional enough, but the chassis underneath was one of that rare and select band to be equipped with two engines. Ford V8 units were used to power all four wheels.

It was hardly more than a party trick for this Land-Rover, but over the years a steady trickle of cars have been either permanently or temporarily adapted for use on rail. In the days when body styles were better suited to such things than the small wheeled, all-enveloping bodywork of today, conversions could be cheap and comfortable means of travel for railway officers.

around the world spend much of their time operating in rough-ground conditions, where the disadvantages of extra weight and mechanical complexity are outweighed by the advantages of good traction.

Another short-lived expedient worthy of mention was the twin-engined lorry. Electric vehicles were occasionally built with separate motors for each driving wheel, the designers thereby avoiding the complication of differential gears: one of the last and oddest was the French-built Sovel of the late 1930s, large – at 8 tonnes capacity – with one motor in front of the rear axle and one behind, and with chain drive to each wheel. But when the practice spread in a very limited way to internal combustion engined lorries, it was because more power was desired than could conveniently be produced by one engine or, more importantly, transmitted by the clutches, gears, and universal joints of the day. In the late 1920s and early 1930s France was more advanced than most nations in terms of vehicle size and speed, so it was perhaps not very surprising that Chenard-Walcker ventured into the complexities of twin-engined (of the sleeve-valve pattern – itself a Lost Cause) twin-transmission lorries with cross-linked controls. That was in 1931, but since the intention was to carry 22 tonnes at no more than 60 km/h, the increase in both unladen weight and complication seemed hardly necessary. Belgium's Miesse did much the same thing at much the same time on a bus of quite ordinary capacity; on a somewhat grander scale there was the American Relay, a double-drive six-wheeler with two engines, two air-controlled gearboxes, and producing about 135 hp.

Later, in post-Second World War years, doubled-up power trains were sometimes found in those enormous trucks used in quarries and on big civil engineering sites. There was also a quite small lorry built by the British Straussler company, which equipped it with a pair of Ford V8 engines, but that was for the Army – one of many strange and exotic things done in the cause of war.

Perhaps the most elusive of all the 'holy grails' sought by transport engineers is a vehicle capable of running at will on road or rail. The difficulties these have met have been very real and, so far, insuperable. Quite apart from the obvious differences between road and rail vehicles, there are subtle but profound differences in the kinds of vibration caused by road surfaces and rail, and traction demands from the long and gentle slopes that characterise railway tracks are very different from those met on the short, sharp and frequent hills of any road journey. Add to those considerations the severely limited distance between rails and the comparatively generous width and height of railway rolling stock, while road vehicles feature narrow bodies and wide track, and it is clear that a truly hybrid vehicle will not be found easily. (Nor, may it be added, will it be much easier to find sufficient applications where such a vehicle would be particularly useful.) Nevertheless, several people have tried. The most successful results have been at the bottom end of the scale, where passenger cars have sometimes had their steering gear locked in the straight-ahead position and their road wheels replaced with a set of the flanged variety: American Jeeps, it was found, were particularly suitable for this kind of rapid conversion, but these were not true road-railers, something that the Karrier of 1930 undoubtedly was.

The Karrier Ro-Railer was sponsored by two of the British main line railway companies, who hoped it might become an acceptable answer to the twin problems of branch line working and permanent way maintenance in remote areas. The crucial feature of the design lay in its wheels which were co-axial, pneumatic tyred and flanged, with the rail ones inside the road. The latter were arranged to slide up into the wheel arches, giving sufficient clearance for the rail wheels and with no risk of fouling points, crossings and other railway track obstructions. In road or rail form the Ro-Railer could run at something like 100 km/h, and changing its mode of progress took about 2½ minutes.

Less enterprising mechanically was an articulated lorry built by the French Willème concern during the early 1930s for road-rail running: in place of the complicated and weighty components of the Karrier, Willème users had to unbolt the road wheels, exposing flanged wheels already in place and ready for work. A simple rail ramp ensured that the rubber tyres carried no weight while being detached or mounted – a procedure that took some time.

Perhaps the most surprising arrangement was that adopted in the mid-1930s by Hendrickson in

America – quite simply, to deflate the roadgoing tyres in order that flanged wheels on the same axles could bear on the rails. One explanation of this dubious-sounding practice is undoubtedly that the one lorry actually built was used by tyre maker B. F. Goodrich.

Karrier, Willème, and Hendrickson were intended for main line working and were certainly interesting; but it turned out that a much more useful application of road vehicles to rail traction lay in the humbler duties of the shunting yard. Railbound motive power compelled to move only over tracks already cluttered with wagons is at its maximum disadvantage in such circumstances – indeed the time-hallowed way of moving wagons in yards was with large horses, although ship-like winches and ropes were sometimes used. Just as soon as rubber tyred versions of Ford-pattern agricultural tractors became available, they were seized upon for shunting purposes where their greater agility and tirelessness made them natural and direct replacements for horses.

Inevitably it was only a matter of time before operators began to cast speculative eyes on rubber tyred vehicles as a means of supplanting not only shunting horses but shunting locomotives, too. Latil, never a company deterred by unconventional engineering, produced a tractor with all four pneumatic tyred wheels driven and steered, and which was much like its standard products for forestry and industrial haulage. But suspended beneath it, fore and aft, were pairs of pressed-steel flanged wheels which could be lowered to rail level, where they acted as guides; all the traction came from the rubber tyres, which ran on the rail heads and carried much of the weight. The great adhesion between rubber and steel, far more than steel on steel, gave the Latil an on-rail performance out of all proportion to its size, not to mention a speed of about 30 km/h, but in its occasional forays on to public roads it looked very strange indeed, with buffer beams, buffers and couplings at each end. A larger version with eight rail wheels appeared in 1937.

During the mid-1960s an American manufacturer returned to much the same idea with a shunting machine which, like the Latil, relied on rubber tyres for carrying and drive, with flanged wheels for

The Daimler-Benz Unimog is another essentially roadgoing tractor that can readily be adapted for rail running. The tiny flanged wheels do no more than guide: all the traction comes from the pneumatic tyres. Latil built several shunting tractors on exactly the same plan.

Left and far left: Karrier built one of the very few truly convertible road-rail machines, and arranged matters so that the rail wheels remained concentric with the bearings while the road wheels could be swung up and out of the way on eccentric mountings. Like many another attempt at such intermodal transport it worked well enough in tests but was not perpetuated. West German railways have tried a trailer using a somewhat similar idea *(above)*, but without the complication of having to transmit power through the wheels.

guidance. The US design, however, had a further ingenious refinement: it would jack itself into the air, turn through a right-angle, lower itself and run off sideways – and could thus escape from between two stationary rail wagons.

Sadly, such attractive diversions can never figure large in the overall scheme of things, and the most successful modern forms of road-rail collaboration are undoubtedly the American Piggy-Back trains, which take advantage of a very generous loading gauge to transport full sized road vehicles, usually semi-trailers, on the main haul part of their journeys. There are similar operations in Europe, notably in Germany.

The nearest thing to a true road-railer now is probably the French Kangourou system, where purpose-built trailers also have rail-style wheels that guide them into place on trains of special railway wagons. Even the Kangourou is not quite as modern as it might seem, for as long ago as

Road on to rail presents one set of problems: a very different lot appear when attempts are made to get rail vehicles on to roads. One real difficulty is weight – railway wagons are built heavily to withstand shunting and other stresses, and if they are to keep within legal roadgoing weight limits their payload is necessarily restricted. Another snag is overall height. Kaelble tried hard to overcome these drawbacks for the German railways during the 1930s, but it is clear that the engineering problems were great.

1931, regular road-rail services using a similar idea began in Britain. Trailer maker Dyson built a fleet of six-wheeled drawbar milk tankers, with capacities of 9,100 litres each, which were pulled on to adapted rail wagons with subsidiary steel wheels engaging guide rails. They ran, with every appearance of success, for many years.

Now, of course, there are the universal and completely intermodal containers, which need no wheels of their own at all. It is a sobering thought that, until 25 years ago, containers might themselves have been described almost as a lost cause, for only then, after more than a century of spasmodic application, did containers quite suddenly blossom into the most exciting development in surface transport since the advent of motor transport itself.

On the whole, it might be wise not to dismiss any currently out-of-favour idea as a Lost Cause, after all.

Rather more success has come from carrying lightly adapted road vehicles aboard rail wagons. Indeed, latter-day operations in central Europe and America use ordinary semi-trailers. In an earlier decade a British railway transported milk tankers on special wagons: the semi-trailers had extra guide wheels fitted for running along the train.

WORKING WITH LORRIES

Generally speaking, the ordinary citizen does not love lorries. Yet there is a growing respect for the men (and nowadays some women, too) who drive them for a living. It is a respect shared by many governments – at any rate those who insist on tests and examinations before issuing the personal licences that allow drivers to take lorries on to public roads.

As in so many other aspects of road transport, there is an enormous variety between the extremities of driving: at one end of the scale are salesmen who carry their wares from shop to shop in vans, and who hardly consider themselves drivers, let alone lorry drivers. At the other end are men capable of making themselves understood in three or more languages, and of dealing with the complications of cross-frontier documentation: they take the great international trucks across Europe and beyond, and might fairly be regarded as top-grade chauffeurs. They form a select elite (a recent development) in their lofty air-conditioned homes-on-wheels; with stereo-cassette radios softly playing, these aristocrats of the driving profession speed along the highways of the world.

Things were very different, once.

It is not easy to decide why so little concern was shown in the early days for the physical comfort of drivers. Granted, until the advent of safety glass it was not easy to provide an enclosed cab: plate glass was sometimes used, but few drivers relished the lapful of broken glass which could result from a minor mishap on the road. Even after windscreens came into general use it was often necessary to drive with them fully opened during fog, snow or heavy rain. Modern motorists are rarely fully aware of how great a blessing is the automatic windscreen wiper: a cut raw potato smeared over the glass – the time-honoured aid to vision in rain – makes a poor substitute.

The absence of any protection worthy of the name for vehicle crews became a time-honoured custom in horse-drawn days, and it continued over the first 20 years or so of motor transport, despite the greater discomfort caused by much higher speeds. Not much more than a token was the folding hood, something which lingered in military circles until the 1940s, although this Scottish-built Halley (right) was built 30 years before then. The American Autocar (far right, top) removed even the minimal screen offered by a conventional bonnet by putting its crew over the engine: pleasant on a sunny day, but . . . Even in Sweden, where people know all about wintry weather, Vabis (far right, bottom) provided only the sketchiest of cab enclosures.

The general absence of full-height side doors in lorry cabs built much before 1930 was in the main a concession to the need for hand signalling, but it was almost impossible to provide much comfort in a cab so poorly protected from the elements. Usually the structure was made of simple wooden boarding, sometimes stained and varnished on the inside, more often painted. The driver and his mate would have nothing better than thin leatherette-covered pads for their seating and more pads of the same kind screwed to the cab rear wall served as backrests. One reason for the seat cushions being removable was that, quite often, they concealed the petrol tank: sometimes, instead, the tank was hung from the dashboard, just above the crews' knees.

Such primitiveness was generally left behind with the adoption of fully enclosed cabs, but the overall standards of comfort, particularly in seating (something of no small moment to men who spend much of their working lives sitting down) remained poor. Until very recent times most makers offered no greater refinement than a simple to and fro sliding adjustment of the driving seat, and even those men who chanced to fit physically into the environment created for them had to stretch and bend a great deal when reaching for the controls. As pressures grew to maximise the revenue-earning part of the vehicles, cabs became increasingly cramped; in the days when drivers sat behind their engines they had at least adequate space. Then came the near-universal move to the forward control, or cab-over layout in heavy vehicles and all at once drivers had to share their living quarters with a large box covering the engine, taking up fully a third of the floor area. At much the same time diesel engines began their all-conquering progress and the unfortunate crews found themselves cramped in a vibrating little kennel, breathing the all-pervading odour of oil fuel, always hot – often unbearably so – and subject to the unending roar of the engine. Indeed, even as late as the early 1970s, heavy lorries were still being built with cabs in which the noise level exceeded that reckoned to cause permanent damage to hearing.

By an odd irony, most of these failings could be laid at the doors of the makers of high quality hand-built vehicles, whose low production outputs made it essential to use standard components (whether home made or bought in) wherever possible, something exacerbated by their willingness to build odd 'special' chassis to individual requirements. A gearbox may have been beautifully made, but its selector lever was in all probability somewhere near the driver's shoulder, and the pedals were offset to one side. In contrast, the American-inspired mass-producers offered draught-free cabs, positioned behind almost silent petrol engines, with instrument and control layouts culled from passenger car practice. Those 3-to-5 tonners of the 1930s and 1940s had many failings, but lack of cab comfort (by contemporary standards) was not one of them.

Redress duly came with the generation of light and medium weight trucks that first saw the light of day during the mid-1960s. They had their cabs positioned squarely over unrefined and very noisy diesels, and even extensive interior lining could do

no more than make them tolerable. A major revolution was overtaking their bigger brothers, however, and every maker seriously intending to stay in the business was soon building veritable palaces on wheels. Cabs became high enough to give a substantially flat floor over front wheels and over new, more powerful engines; standards of trim became at least as good as the best passenger cars, and there was even a change in the all-important matter of seat comfort with the general adoption of suspension seats. Adjustable for rake, height and the occupant's weight, these are carried on springs and dampers in such a way that they form an effective insulation against the lurchings and vibrations of the rest of the vehicle. Even when fitted in older, cruder cabs, suspension seats can make a world of difference to their occupants.

Something else that has done a great deal to improve the status and well-being of lorry drivers is a rapid increase in the number of cabs fitted with good quality sleeping accommodation. It was a development long since pioneered by America, coming into general use as more and more operators ventured on to really long journeys and their crews began to insist on overnight quarters of a better and cleaner standard than so many hostels and dormitories seem able to provide.

Perhaps the most convincing evidence of all that

Cab comfort was not much improved even after doors became regular fittings. No attention at all was paid to such refinements as sealing-in the controls, so that draughts from holes in the floor added to other discomforts. More could have been done with the upholstery, although low speeds made such seating less taxing than it might have been. This is a 'subsidy' Leyland of about 1920.

Once the cab-over, or forward control, style came into fashion, lorry crews had to become accustomed to sharing their working quarters with the engine. It restricted the width available for seating, made life very noisy, and restricted access for maintenance. But, as this late 1930s ERF shows *(right)*, only the minimum of body load space was taken up.

Light and medium weight vehicles, on the other hand, tended to keep their engine bonnets until very recent times. Their cabs, as on this Commer *(far right)*, reflected something of their contemporary mass-produced passenger cars, and since most of them had quiet-running petrol engines, crew conditions were good. Better, faster roads and a growing appreciation of the economics of road transport led to much greater distances being covered by the late 1950s, and standards of cab comfort began to rise dramatically. Henschel *(right, below)* contrived to produce an almost clear floor, with controls and instruments conveniently positioned, and plenty of sound deadening trim fitted to the doors, roof, and framing.

standards of cab comfort are now at a generally acceptable level are the radios and other forms of in-cab electronic entertainment becoming widely adopted. Only two decades ago, in-cab conversations had to be shouted.

Not until 1928 did France, Germany, America and Britain settle on the arrangement of driving controls that is to all intents and purposes now universal. The British had already discovered (in the hard school of war) some advantages of standardisation in components such as tyres, magnetos and spark plugs on their already remarkably uniform subvention lorries, although in the 1912 specification for these vehicles there was thought to be nothing odd in dismissing the accelerator pedal as an optional 'if required' fitting.

It was in their braking arrangements that the earliest commercial vehicles showed maximum diversity, and it would have been a knowledgeable or rash driver who claimed to be familiar with all or even many of them. There was the chain-driven 1908 Stoewer, for example, from a long-forgotten Germany factory, which had two pedals: one for the clutch, which on disengaging also applied one of the brakes on the differential countershaft; and one for the other countershaft brake. The wheel brakes were lever-operated – and also disconnected the clutch. An Italian SPA of much the same period had no less than four separate means of stopping: two pedal-operated on the transmission (one in front of the gearbox, one behind), lever-operated shoes in the rear wheels, and an internal sprag in the back axle casing.

The dubious plan of arranging things so that clutch disengagement preceded brake application was not uncommon (and led to at least one notorious mishap with a Daimler in Britain) and it was quite common to give two totally separate functions to one control. De Dion arranged matters so that as a foot pedal closed the throttle, it also applied the transmission brake. To make doubly sure, the makers pointed out that "the (ignition) switch is close to hand". They made no mention of the explosion in the exhaust system likely to result if the switch was indeed used in the way suggested – perhaps it was felt that such bangs in the silencer were so common in those days of hand-controlled ignition advance and retard that a few more hardly mattered. (Automatic ignition control, responding to pressure fluctuations in the inlet manifold, did not become general until the 1930s.) Even then, Leyland was still making a considerable sales point of

Nowadays very high standards of in-cab comfort are provided, and this Leyland of the 1970s makes a fascinating comparison with its ancestor of 60 years before. Sleeping accommodation, once the preserve of trucks covering the longest distances, is now frequently provided for only occasional use — and deemed a considerable addition to working conditions.

Transmission brakes of one kind or another, once very common fittings, are still sometimes provided. Generally they follow the pattern of this mid-1950s Citroen, where a disc mounted on the propeller shaft is pressed by lined pads. The disc has slots cast in to it, to aid cooling.

its push-on lever for applying the rear wheel drum brakes: while most of the industry were by then used to pulling at their parking brakes, Leyland maintained that pushing effectively added the driver's body weight as a kind of involuntary servo assistance. Good idea or no, it was ultimately abandoned in the interests of standardisation.

As soon as wheel brakes were able to cope with the full demand, transmission brakes fell into disuse, much to the relief of many who dreaded the thought of an over-enthusiastic application proving too much for a universal joint or shaft, upon which the vehicle would lose the steadying influence of the engine. Not many such accidents actually happened, although it was common for transmission brakes to take fire on long descents: wise drivers whose charges possessed the refinement of a water-cooled brake made sure that the dash mounted reservoir was full, with its drip feed into the drum adjusted to a nicety.

Laffly allayed conventional fears by producing a chassis in the early 1930s with a hand-operated transmission brake specifically for holding speed down to safe levels on mountain roads. Latil, a year or two later, made the point even more emphatically with a 12 tonnes capacity six-wheeler which had two hand levers: one applied shoes in the rear drums, the other operated a transmission brake and disengaged the clutch. But that vehicle was

remarkable in other ways, not least for its V8 diesel engine and 100km/h top speed.

Finally, in a spirited defence of the transmission brake right at the end of its period one enthusiast claimed it actually helped promote longer life for driveline components by bringing into use the sides of gear teeth and bearings that would otherwise rarely be used.

For those with eyes to see, however, the Swiss Berna concern had already shown, even before the 1920s were out, the real answer to brake fade on long descents: this was to arrange matters so that, at will, the engine becomes a species of compressor, with artificially increased back-pressure leaving wheel brakes cool, unstressed and ready for their proper purpose. The American Jacobs company devoted a great deal of research to such devices, and the Jake Brake has for decades been a considerable comfort to drivers piloting heavy vehicles in mountainous country.

In earlier times brakes fitted to the countershafts of chain driven vehicles were generally regarded highly for work in heavy traffic, largely because there was less likelihood of dirt and wet interfering with their action, and because the greater speed at which the countershaft revolved gave a smoother action for less driver effort. This being so, it would be interesting to know what contemporary drivers thought of the German Dürkopp, whose side brake (hand lever) applied a self-tightening band brake, which wrapped around a drum. In those early days of road transport, braking efficiency depended largely upon the relative grades of cast iron used for drum and shoe, for there was no lining between them and drivers were expected to make frequent ministrations with an oil can.

Perhaps the greatest godsend with diesel engines for the drivers was that they made provision of starting gear almost essential. This did not happen immediately, for several early makers in the field of oil engines made a point of emphasising the 'ease' with which their products could be started by hand: an unfortunate driver confronted with this task would set a lever which had the effect of halving compression in the cylinders, and spin the starting handle as fast as he could. Then he snapped the lever shut and – with luck – the engine started. On a cold day he might have to enlist the aid of an assistant to hold an oil-soaked burning rag over the air intake, for warmed air can do wonders on cold damp mornings.

This routine, if marginally more exhausting, was at any rate simpler than the ritual necessary for there to be any likelihood of a prompt winter start with the big petrol engines that were destined to be supplanted by those first generation diesels. Lorries invariably used the cheapest petrol available – very low octane stuff – and on a winter morning the

wise driver would drain his carburettor and refill it with higher quality fuel. He, or his mate, would already have put a lighted oil lamp under the sump to warm the lubricating oil. Then, with the ignition switch off, the procedure called for three or four turns on the starting handle to prime the cylinders; set hand throttle lever at one-third open, close the choke (invariably known in those days as the strangler), retard the spark, switch on ignition – and a smart swing should start it. A difficult big engine might well need a rope around the starting handle and two strong men on the rope; another might start every time with no more than a nonchalant kick. Yet no one who heard any of the well-founded stories of terrible injuries inflicted by the starting handles of backfiring engines ever treated lightly the business of starting one, nor were they keen deliberately to stop and have to restart during the day.

Indeed, a major selling point for the first few makers of self-starting equipment was the quantity of fuel that would be saved once drivers were willing to switch off their engines at every stop. In fairness to owners, however, it was not just an urge to prevent unnecessary outlay that held back a widespread adoption of electric starting – although poverty, real or assumed, certainly played a large part: any such scheme also meant using batteries to store electricity and generators to produce it, and neither component was being produced in robust enough form to withstand for long the vibration and hazards of life on a lorry.

There were alternative provisions for starting vehicle engines without having recourse to electricity. Compressed air, stored in a bottle, was tried before the First World War and made occasional appearances thereafter, but its use implied widespread availability of suitable air compressing facilities, for if a driver could get going in one town despite an empty air bottle he could presumably do so in all the others, thereby saving the weight and cost of the equipment. Compressed air certainly found a niche for itself in the field, but its real forte proved to be in starting the really big diesel plants in marine and generator installations.

An indication of just how unsatisfactory electrical starting equipment was in its early days was the somewhat desperate expedient adopted by the British Garrett concern, which tried to sell a heavy duty chassis powered by a weighty, slow speed, Benz-pattern oil engine: this machine had a small (hand-started) petrol engine in the cab which, in turn, started the main diesel. A much more elegant variation on the same theme was offered by the American Hercules engine: it too used a small petrol engine as a starter, but this was mounted neatly on the diesel and connected so that it could also warm the cooling water, lubricating oil, and air manifold in order to lessen its own labours during the actual starting.

As with so many luxuries that soon become necessities, the Americans were first to offer lorries fitted with electric starters and lighting, soon after the 1918 Armistice. With that equipment, and the engine-driven generator required to power them, it was only a matter of time before makers began taking advantage of cheaply and easily made coil and battery ignition. Owners elsewhere fought a

The inverted tooth chain would have done something to refine the transmission generally, but drivers would probably have been more enthusiastic about the brakes fitted to the countershaft. Here they were to some degree protected from mud and wet, while the higher speed at which the countershaft revolved improved the action.

Contemporary approaches to steam power on common roads. The National, sometimes known as Clarkson (above), stemmed from a determined and nearly successful attempt to market steam buses. The designer wisely made his products somewhat 'petrol-like' in their appearance and fired them with paraffin: fuel costs rose to disastrous heights during the First World War and a few of the chassis were converted to coke. Sentinel steamers also burned solid fuel, but the machines were much heavier and more durable than the Nationals – and a great deal more successful commercially, too.

long rearguard action against all these complications, preferring magnetos as the means of producing the sparks necessary for ignition. Drivers very frequently viewed the often erratic magneto with jaundiced eyes, and the knowledgeable among them learnt that in damp weather it was well worth while to leave the troublesome thing overnight in a warm oven (or, when away from home, even to take it into bed) so that no lingering moisture in the windings could cause internal shorts and prevent the essential sparking.

While vehicle speeds were low, owners could claim to be justified in resisting electric lighting, with its added complication of fragile and unreliable bulbs. Paraffin lamps were trouble-free if the wicks were kept clean and the reflectors polished and would burn for up to 20 hours on one filling of oil.

The intensity of illumination was not nearly as good as that from acetylene lighting of course, but acetylene lamps needed attention every four or five hours (although in recompense the frugally-minded soon found that exhausted carbide made an excellent whitewash!).

One real advantage of those old-style lighting systems was the ease with which a headlamp could be taken from its appointed place and used to cast some welcome illumination upon whatever part of the vehicle mechanism happened to be giving trouble. Most on-the-road mishaps were likely to be of the blocked fuel line variety, for there was no guaranteeing the cleanliness or purity of petrol at a time when long distances separated petrol stations, and every driver carried his own reserves in cans.

A particularly annoying ailment was clutch-slip:

the science of making virtually impassable oil seals had a long way to go, and it took very little oil escaping from the crankshaft rear bearing or elsewhere to contaminate the leather lining in a cone clutch. The only real remedy was to cure the leak, dismantle the clutch, thoroughly clean the leather, redress it with neatsfoot oil (or whatever other brew appealed to the mechanic's prejudices) and reassemble. By the roadside, late at night, and with a delivery to make, the clever driver would simply sprinkle some fullers earth – talcum powder might serve – on the leather and with a little luck he would be back on his way.

A really bad case of clutch slip, and a really urgent load, demanded more desperate remedies. One, of last resort, was to insert short lengths of broken hacksaw blade under the lining between the rivets, when the much reduced areas of leather that bore on the flywheel could be guaranteed to grip for a few miles at least. Of one thing vehicle designers and owners might be sure: no driver would willingly slip his cone clutch by foot pressure. The spring loading necessary to transmit engine power through a strip of leather was so great that an aching leg and cramped muscles were inevitable after a day's driving in traffic. Fortunately, low engine and road speeds, with wide-spaced straight toothed gears in the gearbox, meant that most drivers soon cultivated the knack of changing ratios on the move without using the clutch at all. It needed a good ear for engine and gearbox noises, and then it was easy, or so said successful practitioners.

The need to declutch for every change was, in fact, reckoned a grave disadvantage by old hands when more modern transmissions came into being, but by then the diesel engine was beginning its ascendancy, and road speeds were increasing too. Thinking owners and makers began to accept that a wider choice of ratios would make it practicable for drivers to run engines steadily at optimum speed, with less fuel-wasting, even while maintaining higher averages on hilly routes. As an incidental bonus, there would be better engine-braking, too.

An obvious next step was to add an overdrive ratio to the gearbox, so that after reaching top gear,

Passenger car production techniques have brought much to lorry cab designs: provided enough are required to warrant the cost of tooling, good-looking, convenient, and comfortable work places can be made. Quantity is the secret of success, for the price of putting a modern all-steel cab into production is not much less than that for a car. The British Motor Corporation made good use of its considerable expertise in such things when it made the corner-door cab for its trucks *(right, top)*: the door hinged open without projecting beyond the overall width. American manufacturers reached sufficiently high levels of demand long before most others, and nearly a decade of pressed steel cabs preceded this Chevrolet of 1939 *(right, below)* – itself 20 years older than the BMC.

Different places, different priorities. It is almost unbelievable that only five years separate the newly introduced AMO of 1931 *(left, top)* and the White of 1936 *(left, below)*. But the AMO was Russian, and neither style nor comfortable cabs were high on their list of requirements for lorries. The White, on the other hand, was clearly designed to sell in a market bewildered by choice.

which is almost invariably 'straight through', with no reduction, the driver could select another ratio which had the effect of reducing engine speed for a given road speed, or allowing the vehicle to run faster without overtaxing the engine. Such overdrives are common enough on passenger cars and light commercials, usually in the form of an auxiliary unit arranged to 'split' the top two conventional ratios, and engaged at will by an electric switch.

Some heavy lorries during the 1930s were fitted with an auxiliary gearbox, usually containing two ratios: by manipulating them, a driver could, in theory, get eight speeds from a basic four-ratio transmission (first lower, first upper, and so on).

Unfortunately, the spread of ratios was usually such that two or more were so close together that awkwardly large gaps were created – quite apart from having two gearchange levers to use – and the same problem arose when two-speed axles (which effectively incorporated a two-speed splitter in the final drive assembly) were used. The ultimate solution came in gearboxes and axles designed to meet the new operating conditions, and while modern drivers may discuss the relative merits of range-change and splitter, they no longer have any difficulty in choosing ratios suitable for their needs, or engaging them.

Clutch design also advanced – and there was a

great deal of room for improvement, for attempts in earlier times to produce the performance and refinement nowadays taken for granted led to a whole range of problems. Multi-plate clutches, in which the metal plates had to run in an oil bath, were a good example: if the oil was too thick, disengagement might well be impossible; too thin, and there was no drive. Since every driver had his own preferences, those who were allowed to exercise such responsibility adjusted the proportions of engine oil and paraffin in the clutch housing to suit their personal driving techniques. Meanwhile, the dry multi-plate fabric-lined clutches favoured by some American makers showed an inclination to seize solid if simply left overnight after a long run in rain. Drivers rapidly learnt to provide themselves with a piece of wood whose length was just enough to jam between seat edge and depressed clutch pedal, and thus keep the plates separated.

In passing, another American export, chewing gum, could sometimes be an unmitigated blessing: it was splendid stuff for sealing leaks in fuel tanks and petrol cans.

Not, of course, until the advent of pneumatic

tyres did readily detachable wheels become common, or even necessary. When they did, there was an immediate divergence of opinion which is with us still: American makers and users took to their hearts the type of wheel in which a spoked centre stays on the axle and just the tyre and rim assembly is removed, while Britain almost unanimously favoured pressed steel wheels bolted to a hub assembly that usually incorporated the brake drum. The rest of Europe leaned toward American practice for heavy vehicles and one-piece wheels for smaller ones, reasoning that a large tyre and rim was quite enough to manhandle without adding any more metal to the weight. If nothing else, detachable rim wheels minimise the dangers of inadvertently using incompatable nuts on the studs of one-piece wheels, an error easily made and one that even now occasionally leads to tragic results.

Perhaps the American fondness for detachable rims even on lighter commercial vehicles stemmed (at least in part) from their attachment to wooden wheels, long after the rest of the world had abandoned them. Nicely varnished spokes looked very well indeed, local manufacturers seemed to have no difficulty in finding ample supplies of suitable hardwoods, and they extolled the shock-absorbing qualities of their products. Wary drivers meanwhile learnt to listen for the characteristic creaking sounds emitted by a wooden wheel whose joints were beginning to loosen, and to do something about it – quickly. A sensible man kept a close eye on his wooden wheels, particularly during hot weather, when he could save himself a great deal of trouble by draping water-soaked sacks over the spokes during any halt of more than a few minutes. Linseed oil, well rubbed in, was generally considered a worthwhile treatment and, even when the wheels were shod with rubber, no driver in his senses would drive at speed over stone-block paving or any other vibration-inducing surface.

Drivers whose charges were fitted with cast steel spoked wheels needed to do no more than lightly tap each spoke once a week or so, on the same principle that railway rolling stock examiners still tap wheels: there is no easier way of detecting faults than to hear and recognise the clear ringing tones given out by sound spokes from the dull flat note from a cracked one.

Once solid rubber tyres became established, their makers set up service depots at which the most important pieces of equipment were large hydraulic presses capable of pressing off an old tyre from the rim and pressing on a new one, for the interference fit between the tyre backing band and the wheel played an important part in holding them together. While it lasted, a solid rubber tyre would not give much trouble, although there was always a risk that a too-close encounter with a kerbstone or half-brick might chip out a lump of the unreinforced rubber, whereafter the inescapable clop, clop, clop, noise emitted by the damaged tyre acted as a constant reminder to the driver of his carelessness. To be sure, operating circumstances were clearly reflected in tyre condition, then as now. Solids on urban buses, running over fairly smooth surfaces and rarely turning fast enough to generate destructive heat, wore down evenly almost to the backing band (the shock-absorbing abilities disappearing

Apart from a lingering fondness for two-piece windscreens with extra corner-pieces, there is little in common between these DAF cabs of 1951 *(left)* and 1966 *(below)*. The former served well enough when DAF found most of its customers in The Netherlands, but as its exporting ambitions grew, cabs better suited to long distance international running had to be provided.

at a rate strictly proportional to the wear); the comparatively long fast journeys made by lorries could easily soften the rubber enough to make it susceptible to damage by any stone.

Tyre changing in the solid rubber era was, however, not a frequent chore, although conscientious owners would keep one set of wheels with smooth tread (more durable) tyres for summer work and another equipped with one of the many 'skidproof' patent tread patterns for winter. Whatever their slip-resisting propensities, the latter always cost more and lasted less, hence the need to change. Until the road-building programmes of the 1920s got under way, of course, motor vehicle operation in many parts of the world was very much a climatic affair: and the snow, mud and cold of winter could easily stop long-distance work, a state of affairs forgotten in more favoured regions since the eighteenth century.

Despite their many advantages it was inevitable that pneumatic tyres would also bring some dis-advantages. One was cost, compounded by the frequency with which the new equipment needed attention. Punctures were frequent at first – contemporary hazards now quite gone included horse-shoe nails lurking on the stony-surfaced roads, not to mention razor-edged flints – and a driver faced with the job of making roadside repairs could not be regarded as a fortunate man. There would probably be a spare wheel, something which no solid tyred vehicle ever possessed, and the more thoughtful chassis makers included a little winch or other means of lowering the spare from its resting place to the ground. Even then it was heavy work to unbolt a wheel, lift it off the mounting studs, lift on the spare, secure it, and get the punctured tyre and wheel back into the 'spare' rack. A lorry driver on journey work would then have to find a garage willing to repair the puncture while he waited, for to go any further than necessary without a fit spare was to court disaster, and owners tended to take a poor view of desperate or over-resourceful drivers who, faced with an irreparable puncture, stuffed the expensive casing with rope or straw and carried on.

There was much debate in the earliest days of pneumatics about the relative advantages of large-section singles, which were very heavy, and smaller tyres mounted as twins – apt, then as now, to trap damaging stones between their sidewalls. Arranging tyres in tandem, as on six-wheeled chassis, led to the rearmost casings suffering more than their fair share of punctures, caused by nails thrown up by the tyres immediately in front. Another difficulty was the relative scarcity of inflating equipment able to handle the high pressures used in the new tyres. Some vehicle makers, notably in America, thoughtfully provided gearbox-driven compressors; French engineers leaned towards highly compressed air in bottles. Ultimately, of course, patience had its reward, and despite constant entreaties from the makers to use their products with a measure of consideration, one of the last things to worry the average modern lorry driver is the durability of his tyres. And when a failure does come, gone are the days of struggling with recalcitrant wheel nuts and rusty, muddy, spare wheel carriers; instead, a telephone call brings a breakdown tender and specialist tyre fitter, complete with exchange wheels, from one of the many tyre servicing networks.

The modern driver is even less likely to think about the condition of the final drive on his vehicle, but in chain-driven days only the irresponsible neglected this essential component. At the very least it was worth a daily kick at each chain to see if it was becoming dangerously slack, because an over-loose chain could easily jump off its sprocket while running downhill, effectively removing any braking effort from the engine or countershaft drums. It was usually a simple enough matter to adjust a pair of screwed radius links that located the rear axle, and thereby move the axle a little forward or backward in the chassis. A longer job (for careful owners) came about once a year, when the rear wheel assemblies, including the chain wheels, were exchanged side for side. This had the effect of evening wear on the teeth, which could easily become unacceptably hooked under the grinding influence of road dust mixed with lubricating oil.

The use of roller chains led to another irksome chore, the need to take them off the vehicle every five or six weeks and soak them in a mixture of tallow, graphite and oil – ideally, boiling them in it. The oil soaked into all the many clearances to be found in a large roller chain which, after this treatment, gave the impression of having shrunk in length. This of course meant going through the business of moving the axle forward, and then back again in instalments, as the lubrication squeezed out.

One real advantage of chain final drive was the ease with which the hill climbing ability and top speed could be altered, even at the roadside, by simply changing the countershaft chainwheels for others with more or fewer teeth. It is not hard to imagine the joy with which some rogue drivers realised they had within their grasp the means of obtaining rather more spectacular increases in speed: by removing one final drive chain altogether, and securing the countershaft chain-wheel on that side to prevent it revolving, the differential action had the effect of making the other side turn twice as fast!

Nearly everyone today has at least some idea of how a motor vehicle functions, but the generation which understood the mysteries of earning a living by driving steam on common roads is now all but gone. Steam men had much to occupy their minds: the prime worry was maintaining the correct water level in the boiler; too much, and water carried over with the steam might damage the engine; too little, and boiler plating exposed to the fire with no water backing to conduct away the heat might buckle, giving rise to expensive repairs. Even an apparently safe quantity of water in the locomotive-style boiler of an overtype might not be enough to keep the vulnerable firebox crown covered during a steep descent.

That was not a problem shared by undertypes with their vertical boilers, but the undertype driver was constantly preoccupied with getting and keeping a sufficient volume of steam. For a boiler does not only generate steam, it also stores it until required by the engine, and vertical boilers had much less volume than those of the locomotive type.

Finding water to put in the boiler was, to a driver travelling on unfamiliar roads, likely to cause nail-biting anxiety. In some places water was available from town mains, often by means of something akin to the agency cards used by modern lorry drivers to obtain fuel. Elsewhere, a clear running stream was the favoured source, although no more than necessary was taken in 'hard' water districts, because of the resulting deposits that would have to be scraped from inside the shell on boiler wash-out day. And no steamer driver would ever take water from a duck pond except in desperation: the personal habits of ducks are such that the water would soon foul any boiler.

Steam wagon design became quite refined as the years went by and a useful degree of automation crept into the business of steam generation, but in earlier times there was simply too much for one man to manage on his own. Even with two men in the cab, both had quite enough tasks to keep them busy, and the minute by minute fluctuations in traffic conditions demanded a great deal of skill and mutual understanding by both men if the driver was to have enough steam to negotiate an unexpected hill, if the fireman was to have enough suitable water when the tanks needed filling, and if both were to avoid prosecution for "permitting visible steam or smoke" in a town, or even a charge of manslaughter should the boiler explode with fatal results. In the far-off days when the driver was responsible for everything but the steering, teamwork was even more essential if hilarious (and occasionally disastrous) *contretemps* were not to result.

But steamer driving had its compensations: there was unlimited hot water for washing, for tea or coffee – and nothing in the world tasted better than steak, bacon, herring, or eggs grilled to perfection on a shining shovel over a clean fire while trundling slowly along a quiet country road.

By dint of cleverly combining a collection of standard components the Leyland group found it was able to adapt its 'Ergonomic' cab of the 1960s to vehicles intended for very different purposes. Mounted high, above the front wheels *(left)*, it offered sufficient space and potential comfort for long distance haulage, and a sleeper extension could be added *(as the picture on page 121 shows)*. Lowered, to bring the cab floor nearer the ground *(centre)*, it formed a spacious work place for drivers who have to climb in and out many times a day.

Inevitably, since all manufacturers are faced with much the same problems, lorry cabs come more and more closely to resemble each other. And, since providing variety and choice becomes ever more expensive, makers — and buyers — are no longer willing to insist upon standards of trim once traditional to the carrying of some cargoes. The building trades, for one, once attracted only the barest of essentials in their lorry cabs; now the driver of a heavy tipper or transit concrete mixer has standards of comfort equalling those of his colleagues engaged on long distance work.

The international face of transport: a Dutch-built DAF hauling a French-made excavator, in Britain *(above)*. The immense and continuing growth in cross-frontier trading has compelled nations in Western Europe to standardise the most important aspects of their laws controlling road transport.

The high cost – and scarcity – of labour has compelled operators to seek more rapid ways of loading and unloading. A big step forward was the general purpose small hydraulically-powered crane, usually mounted just behind the cab and sometimes on the tractor chassis of an articulated vehicle. The Leyland *(right)* adapted to carry building blocks, has a crane halfway along its deck so that all of the cargo can be reached without an excessively long boom. A remarkable example of cross-frontier trading is the Rumanian-built Roman *(opposite)* made under licence from the West German MAN concern, and one of the very few eastern block commercials to sell in the west.

GOOD SERVANTS, POOR NEIGHBOURS

During the years soon after the turn of the century, when road transport was taking its first uncertain steps, the legislation with which it had to comply was at best sketchy. At worst, it also varied from place to place, and the very few operators who tried to provide services across what were often irrelevant boundaries found themselves facing bewildering and contradictory rules, set down and administered with zeal by local dignitaries jealous of their powers. On a large scale the problem is still with us, as inter-state hauliers in Australia, America, Western Europe and elsewhere know full well.

There is an odd aspect to the lorry, always useful and latterly indispensable: it is unwanted by most ordinary citizens. Aeroplanes, railways, ships – all have somehow succeeded in capturing and holding public imagination. Not so the lorry, at whose door is laid the blame for many of the ills to which modern urban man is heir. This universal antipathy has its uses: when something is absolutely essential, and not generally liked, it forms a perfect source of tax revenue. This truism was grasped very quickly indeed, almost as soon as lorries came into general use.

From the very beginning there has been a great deal of concern at the damage a lorry can do to its surroundings, particularly the roads it uses, and mandatory speed limits and taxation – the traditional means of keeping it within bounds – are still relied upon today, with a fair measure of success. But it has also long been held that unbridled road transport causes great harm to other modes of transport, and here the methods adopted in attempting to confine the thrusting intruder have been many, varied and in the main useless. This aspect of the lorry is not entirely unconnected with the third main area in which road transport has often been at variance with the rest of society – its role as an employer.

Most of the conflicts come about from the peculiar nature of the industry, for it is full of contradictions. In order to make universal door-to-door collections and deliveries lorries must be allowed the freedom of virtually every street, no matter how unsuitable for large vehicles some of them may be: this mode of transport cannot be kept at arm's length like every other. At once lorries must face their next irreconcilable dilemma: large vehicles can obviously take large cargoes and thus operate more economically than smaller ones, but if there is one thing in a busy street more objectionable than a large lorry, it is an even bigger one.

The contradictions continue in the matter of ownership. Since in most countries road transport carries 50 per cent or more of manufactured goods, this industry is clearly a vital part of any national economy. Yet, unlike every other essential service industry, it contains few monopolies – far from it; in order to provide the instantaneous response which has made it so dominant, control and ownership must be highly fragmented. Accepted wisdom suggests that it is counterproductive to operate fleets of more than 70 or 80 vehicles, and those companies which own more are usually careful to divide them into operating units of about that size. Often, the most effective service of all is provided by owner-drivers, or by companies owning only three or four lorries.

Couple this with the low profit margins that have always been part of the road transport business, and it follows that it has all too often been a less than satisfactory employer. Working conditions were notoriously poor until the last two generations of heavy vehicle cab designs. In earlier times, to men graduating from the even worse privations accepted in horse-drawn transport, the first motors were probably a positive improvement, but while most of industrial societies bettered such conditions as working hours, canteens, washing facilities and the like, many lorry drivers were encouraged or compelled to work excessive hours and were otherwise left to fend for themselves. An added injustice not shared by most workpeople was the disgracefully poor overnight accommodation endured by drivers engaged in long-distance operations. Matters were not helped in the least by the large numbers of self-employed men willing to put up with the same degree of overwork and hardships in order to establish their own businesses: this is a problem far from solved even now, but for the last half-century an important pre-occupation of all civilised states when framing new road transport law has been the control of exploitation by, and of, the industry itself.

Germany tried repression before retreating into co-operation. In 1925 hauliers were compelled to obtain route authorisations for each state in which they wished to operate, to observe a fixed tariff based on rail charges, and their freedom of movement was limited to a 50 km radius from base, measured along railway routes. Within ten years it had all changed, and while every German haulier was still compelled to join one national association,

which policed a uniform tariff based on railway rates, the road transport industry was freed of direct railway interference in its affairs – although the new and generally admired Autobahnen were originally under railway supervision.

Perhaps the most extraordinary manifestation of German state interest and interference in road transport came a few weeks before war erupted in 1939 when, for its own purposes, the government decided to reduce the number of separate vehicle models in production. The reduction was drastic and remarkable: instead of 113 types only 19 were to suffice; overall, including all kinds of motor vehicle, 335 types were to be rendered down to 81. War intervened before manufacturers, their suppliers and their dealer networks had time to digest this peculiar scheme.

France showed the way ahead in several ways.

An unfortunate mishap – of a kind calculated to bring the maximum amount of unfavourable publicity to lorry transport. Yet the real reason such things happen is that the road structure is not able to carry the load.

Somewhat disconcertingly, as civil aeroplanes became bigger, the lorries which served them found that loading hatches got further out of reach. Some kind of intermediate lift machine would be timewasting and cumbersome, but an effective solution was the scissors lift *(far left)*, in which pairs of sturdy links between chassis and van floor live up to their name by raising the body vertically to whatever height is required. Insulated bodywork is used whenever a cargo must be transported at a controlled temperature – usually, but not inevitably, lower than ambient. The duration of delivery runs must be timed so that temperature change does not exceed the limits laid down *(above)*. All-round unrestricted access for loading and unloading, coupled with fully enclosed bodywork, seemed an almost unattainable ideal until the 'curtain sided' designs evolved *(left)*. The reinforced plastics side sheets can be rolled completely away, or stretch-fastened into place to form sides able to withstand quite heavy movements.

Perhaps the major health hazard in any big town until the mid-1920s was disease-harbouring dust and mud from the streets. Eventually properly sealed road surfaces and motors removed the causes of the dirt; before then the only effective palliative was frequent washing. Paris authorities turned early to motor water wagons using, among others, this Laffly sprinkler *(above, right)*. At much the same time – just before the First World War – Vienna tried an idea that was ultimately discarded: this outsize vacuum cleaner *(below)*. Its task was to remove street refuse without raising clouds of dust, but quite soon the still-familiar rotary brush sweepers showed they could do the job more effectively.

In a move that accurately reflected a growing trend in public opinion, the authorities in Paris were considering proposals to forbid horse traffic on the streets – on public health grounds. Perhaps more significantly, by the end of the 1920s long-distance haulage was well established, with an emphasis on night trunk operations working to fixed timetables. Running speeds were high, and widespread disre-

gard of official limits led, first, to averages of more than 50 km/h and, in 1932, to a rise in the official limit to 65 km/h for 11·2 tonnes gross vehicles (on pneumatics) and to 45 km/h for those grossing 15·7 tonnes. The number of vehicles increased rapidly too, with a national fleet of 366,000 in 1930 growing by 45,500 in 12 months. In a somewhat curious move, the French government charged only half-rate tax for vehicles more than nine years old – and 28 per cent of owners took advantage of it.

The Netherlands land reclamation schemes meant that the Dutch had to deal with 'new lands' and during the later 1930s they began to designate their roads as A, the main highways, and B, the latter suitable only for weights of up to 240 kg on each wheel. Very sensibly they also imposed a maximum vehicle width of 2·1 m – so much easier to police than weight.

Italy in the 1930s was becoming highly politicised and, in addition to making the trains run on time, Mussolini sought to encourage road transport by the markedly unusual step of allowing buyers three tax-free years for vehicles with locally produced oil engines. Anyone who bought an ex-army vehicle could claim the same bounty and the scheme presumably worked, for in 1934 it was extended to permit five-year tax exemptions for buyers of pro-ducer gas vehicles, on which there was also a small government-paid subsidy.

Even without such encouragement, and with generally poor roads, South African inter-urban freight transport grew explosively from its beginnings during the mid-1920s, so thoroughly frighten-

Africa has made something of a speciality of the combined vehicle – half bus, half lorry. Based usually on heavy duty multi-wheel drive lorry chassis, these machines have proved themselves sufficiently durable to withstand 'roads' that would be considered impassable in less arduous surroundings. Rhodesian Railways used these sturdy Leylands to link places that would otherwise have been quite isolated.

ing the state-owned railway system that the government introduced legislation sufficiently repressive to ensure that by 1930 the roads were again empty. But not for long, and the lorries soon returned – this time fostered by the railway authorities.

Argentina, a country with a sparse population living in rural communities that could be hundreds of kilometres from their nearest railheads, was for many years dogged by road construction problems. The Argentines took enthusiastically to heavy motors despite possessing little stone or other material suitable for road building. Argentine roads were poor indeed, often as much as 15 m wide in the hope that drivers would thereby be able to pick their way between the notorious mudholes. Rigid six-wheeled vehicles were thought to be the only answer, and for years Argentina was a steady market for European makers, who could sell similar machines to their colonies.

In some countries, legislation to control the growth of lorry traffic became draconian. In Australia during the years between the two World Wars, the gross weight of a four-wheeled vehicle and its load could not exceed 10 tonnes at a time when Britain, then still very much the Home Coun-

try, permitted 12 tonnes gross and 8 tonnes axle weight; in some areas, Australian six-wheelers could go to 13 tonnes, but both limits seemed meagre compared with the weights then common in Europe and America, particularly since they were accompanied by low legal speeds, high taxes and quite reasonable roads. Matters in the Australian state of Queensland reached an extraordinary pitch during the later 1930s, when a railway-dominated transport board had the authority to refuse or ignore applications to register road vehicles, or to cancel existing registrations, without notice or appeal. But Australia is a country perfectly suited to road transport and traffic continued to grow: New South Wales enjoyed the benefits of regular 350 km trunk haulage services before 1920, and in the four years between 1926 and 1930 the number of horse-drawn goods vehicles in Melbourne halved.

Meanwhile, operators in New Zealand faced a bewildering array of restrictions that included gross vehicle weight limits ranging from 2·5 to 10·2 tonnes, and from 4·6 to 15·2 tonnes for those on three axles. Clearly the preoccupation here, as in many other young countries, was the damage

As early as the late 1920s growers found advantages in sending animals to the Chicago stock yards by road – despite Chicago being the centre of a great railway network. Vehicles adapted for the work provided rapid and reliable service, subjecting their unfortunate cargoes to the minimum of stress-inducing travel. This double-drive Hendrickson has a double-decked body.

Regulations and operating conditions combine to demand different solutions to apparently similar problems. The Bedford *(right)* is a straightforward 4 by 2 tractor hauling an ordinary tandem-axle semi-trailer; in order to maximise capacity, the Fiat *(below)* has an extra pair of wheels, arranged to steer, just behind its front axle; the Scania *(far right)*, faced with similar problems, is again a standard 4 by 2 unit — but its semi-trailer has three axles.

heavily laden lorries could inflict on hastily and inadequately built roads.

The greatest single grievance nursed by rival systems against the road transport industry, however, is that somehow it contrives to charge less than it should for the services it provides, and that to do so comprises unfair competition. This argument preoccupied the mid-1930s National Recovery Administration in America which tried, for a year or two, to enforce its Code for Trucking. The heart of this was compulsory registration of rates by hauliers, with those who seemed to be charging prices that were too low instructed to adopt the price structures of their competitors. It made no real difference. Authority had great difficulty in enforcing registration and – even where it did – in getting operators to charge more, and customers to pay more, than they mutually thought necessary. The industry was too big and growing too quickly for it to be controlled in such a way: from about 20,000 vehicles in 1911 it leapt to 1·2 million in 1921 and to 3·5 million in 1930. The trend was irreversible, and never again would America have to admit, as it did during the First World War, that lack of suitable transport meant more than half of the nation's farm produce could not be got to market.

In passing, the business of getting food animals to market had some fascinating sidelights: according to one calculation, if five bullocks walked 8 km there would be a total weight reduction between them of 100 kg. Another claimed that old-style drovers, constantly diverting from the straight and narrow path in their efforts to keep their wayward charges in order, had to walk twice the nominal distance on a journey. The growth of livestock-carrying by motor not only gave access to a much greater choice of markets, but also, it appears, saved a great deal of meat and boot leather.

The great difficulty for lawmakers everywhere is enforcement. It is relatively simple to enforce an acceptable degree of observance of speed limits and vehicle weight regulations, but it has always been very difficult to tell when a driver has worked an excessive number of hours – particularly when he may well be conniving at the offence. In any case, there is a genuine dispute about what consti-

tute maximum safe working hours and adequate rest, particularly since no such restrictions are placed on the drivers of passenger cars, and unless the necessity and equity of any law is generally accepted it will always be very difficult to enforce. In the end, some form of self-policing is inevitable, with heavy penalties for detected infringements. One acceptably effective system involves work-sheets compiled by each driver and detailing his movements, with both secret and official roadside checks by enforcement officers. More useful is the recording instrument known as the tachograph, which has a respectably long history going back to pre-First World War years. This device is fitted in the vehicle cab and records against a time scale every stop, start, and speed change the driver makes. A measure of the controversy that surrounds the whole question of working conditions and hours for lorry drivers is that while German drivers insisted on tachographs as a defence against exploitation, British drivers have long refused to tolerate them – for the very same reason.

Generally, however, matters have changed considerably for the better in recent years, and the big, fast, modern trucks, with their international image, have given rise to a new kind of driver who is paid well and not disposed to endure the real hardships of his predecessors.

On the face of it, it seems absurd to have to provide a full-time custodian for every consignment of cargo, particularly when loads are often almost valueless – sand, gravel, ashes and so on – while competing transport modes do not: compare the relative carrying capacities and crews of trains, ships, and barges. But once again the apparent weakness is a strength, for with a man to every lorry a simple telephone call is enough to re-route each individual consignment, from small package to 20 tonnes of coal or cattle; to change collection and delivery times; to find suitable return loads for otherwise empty vehicles.

Only individual control can provide such flexibility; even for those commodities which are generated and consumed in large quantities, small consignment transport can often outperform apparently cheaper and more efficient bulk carrying alternatives. If, for example, a factory requires 1,000 tonnes of raw material a week, and there is suitable rail access at both the producing plant and the customer, it may be economic to organise one rail transported delivery a week. But that also presupposes that the manufacturer is prepared to store the whole consignment until it is collected, and that the customer can hold the material until he wants to use it. What is more, if the material has a high intrinsic value, the amount of capital tied up during all this time may well be a serious financial drain.

If, on the other hand, a fleet of lorries is used for transport, a timetable can easily be arranged so that material is delivered just as it is required, and the only holding space needed is a parking area for an hour or two. In a real sense, expensive warehousing can be abolished or much curtailed because lorries moving along the road have become the storage – indeed, often the packing cases too: perhaps 50 collections and deliveries in place of one, yet they are effectively cheaper and more efficient.

Opinions differ very sharply indeed about investment practice within road transport, for again the pattern of contradictions that is so much a part of the industry is to the fore. Measured in terms of return on capital it is not, on the whole, a profitable activity, and it is probably not too extravagant to claim that most of the people in it stay because they love the way of life. So there is a strong incentive to keep capital equipment – which really means the vehicles – for a long time. Against this is a constantly changing infrastructure: legal restraints of all kinds alter quite frequently, and apparently minor changes to permitted speeds or working

It is very hard to visualise life in any modern community without the services of those indispensable lorries, the refuse collecting vehicles. Despite the more economical working possible with horses used over short distances, motors soon began to infiltrate urban operations, and a great deal of ingenuity has gone into developing bodywork for specific purposes. One authority combined the advantages of articulation, and the three-wheeled Karrier tractors more usually found in railway yards, and produced a straightforward collector (opposite, top). The rear part of the body tipped, and was used for household refuse; the front portion carried waste paper. Even the nature of refuse changes with the years, and where once a simple lorry-like body served to carry ashes and similar waste, the lightweight and bulky plastics and paper packaging of modern times demand something more elaborate. Hydraulically operated rams compress the load forward in this Dodge-mounted machine (opposite, centre): to discharge, the whole of the rear hinges upwards and rams push out the compacted load. A worrying trend in most urban communities is the rapid disappearance of suitable dumping sites for refuse, and much longer journeys have to be made. Rubbish generating points spread ever wider, too. In this design of collector (opposite, bottom), vehicle-mounted lifting gear raises purpose-made bins – which are suitable for hotels, hospitals, and the like – and empties them into itself. Long, fast, on-road trips to disposal sites can be made. While the nature of domestic and similar wastes change, so do those from industry; and many unspeakable by-products, capable of causing death or injury in a variety of ways, must be disposed of safely and at minimum cost. After all, waste of any kind is implicitly of no or low value. The 'flying banana' (above) is one operator's answer to the problem of transporting noxious liquids. The curious shape gives a satisfactorily low discharge point for the cargo, and a low centre of gravity. The robust shell is calculated to prevent leakage in the event of road accident.

America led the world in forcing the wholly desirable development of tilt cabs: as the White *(far left, upper and lower)* shows, it is possible to provide excellent access to the chassis components while at the same time leaving the cab interior untouched. That other great advance in living standards for drivers, the sleeper cab, was also an American preoccupation long before the rest of the world realised how useful it could be. Somewhat more generous dimensional allowances made it possible for General Motors to put a sleeper that would seem spacious indeed to Europeans on a 6 by 4 tractor *(above)* and a similar American willingness to make cabs high, wide and handsome is shown by the Mack *(below)*.

143

If there is no one there to annoy, even the largest lorry won't be a nuisance. In northern Sweden, where the population is sparse and many roads are unsealed and gravel-surfaced, lorries of prodigious size and weight operate satisfactorily and hold together a local economy that would otherwise be hard to sustain.

hours can cause profound effects on large sections of the industry, and may well require quite different types of vehicle to meet the altered conditions.

The manufacturing side of road transport is also heavily fragmented and very competitive, and individual makers use all the marketing wiles so familiar in consumer goods industries to persuade users to buy their latest models. It is probably safe to say that no operator likely to stay in business has vehicles more than ten years old, and that most are sold out of service by their fifth birthday, which may well approximate to 400,000 km, for it is at about that length of service that a top quality, or premium, truck begins to need extensive overhauling. A wise owner will try to dispose of his vehicles still earlier, in order to maximise their value on the second-hand market.

Given the short operating life and high initial cost, there is every incentive for owners to keep vehicles busy, and when the high costs of road-usage taxation, vehicle insurance and the servicing of purchase loans are taken into account, it is clear that the financial pressures are considerable.

So lorries are large and noticeable, and because they share the roads with every class of traffic it is difficult to ignore them. Other road users, observing that lorries appear to flourish while state-owned

railway systems require bigger and bigger subsidies, are inclined, not unreasonably, to believe dark rumours of all-powerful road transport lobbies, bringing irresistable pressures to bear in favour of more and more roads and still bigger lorries. In truth, the highly fragmented nature of the industry is such that any kind of sustained concerted action is unlikely, and resistance on a political level to pressures applied by genuinely monolithic competitors is usually feeble. On a commercial plane, matters are very different, but it can fairly be said that road transport has succeeded in spite of, rather than because of, the attitudes adopted towards it by national authorities.

It must be admitted, of course, that governments have, or should have, a somewhat wider view of national economics and well-being than the average haulier, and that governments are generally either the proprietors of rival transport modes or important providers of financial support to them – quite often both. In the event, nearly all law relating to commercial road transport is initiated by government and to some degree is oppressive, for only rarely does the special pleading of operators and their trade associations have more than a marginal effect; no government in its right mind, however, frames new transport law without first consulting

very closely with those who face the prospect of meeting its requirements.

The comprehensive and bewildering rules that govern the construction of vehicles omit virtually no detail of any mechanically propelled transport for use on public roads, and it is a remarkable tribute to designers that they still achieve such lack of uniformity among their products. The seemingly infinite variety of goods to be carried helps in creating much of this diversity: length, width, and in most countries (although Britain is an exception) height are strictly governed and while one maximum dimension is adequate for width and height, permitted lengths vary with the vehicle configuration, which in turn usually varies according to use: a rigid six- or eight-wheeled lorry must generally be longer than a four-wheeler if it is to offer any advantage in transporting a given commodity. But bulk is not the same thing as weight, and a three-axled tipper intended for carrying wet sand may very well have to be shorter than a four-wheeled van used to transport furniture; legal limits on gross vehicle weights, and the maximum weights that may be imposed on individual axles, must be permuted with the allowed distances between axle centres. These complications result from an understandable desire by civic authorities to minimise

damage to road paving and bridges: research has shown, as one would expect, that the more wheels there are under a load, and the more evenly they are spaced, the better. This logic has been taken to visibly absurd lengths by the state legislature in Michigan, which insists on a format that puts ten or more axles under articulated lorries of quite unexceptional length and capacity.

Indeed, operators across state boundaries in what is, in this regard at any rate, a strangely un-United States have had to contend with remarkable regulatory complications: in neighbouring Kentucky and Indiana, for example, maximum permissable gross weights are 36·3 tonnes and 33·2 tonnes; and owners of interstate trucks have difficulty finding space on their vehicles to mount all the separate state registration number plates they are required to carry. Western Europe is no better – albeit for more readily understandable historic reasons – and a great deal of inefficiency results from the present political inability to come to terms with, for example, maximum axle weights of 12·2 tonnes in Italy, 10 tonnes in Denmark, Germany, and Holland, 10·16 tonnes in Britain and Ireland, and 13 tonnes in Belgium, Luxembourg, and France, coupled with maximum gross vehicle weights of, respectively, 44, 38, 32 and 38 tons

There is nothing quite like a 'Michigan monster' anywhere else. Despite the extraordinary number of wheels under it, this double bottom has a gross weight of about 69 tonnes.

(44·7, 38·6, 32·5 and 38·6 tonnes).

But in transport as in other things Europe is something of a special case: if the separate states of America, Australia and South Africa are accepted as identifiable parts of already unified countries, the nations of the European Economic Community are the only real example in modern times of so many disparate and traditionally antagonistic peoples coming together in a determined attempt to form an interdependent federation. Road transport is totally accepted as an inevitable and vital force in this knitting together of Western Europe; but national instincts are still strong and many years will pass before European hauliers obey uniform regulations and compete on a uniform basis.

Something else that seems likely to continue for a long time is the political division of Europe as a whole into two uneasy and mutually suspicious political camps, one committed to something approaching free enterprise capitalism in the ownership and control of its road transport, the other quite different. In practice, the main hindrances to the not-inconsiderable trans-Iron Curtain traffic which already exists are the peculiarly nationalistic pattern of restrictions and controls common throughout Europe and intended to protect local hauliers, or state railways, or roads and bridges, by reducing the number of through movements. The matter is made more complicated by the fact that several central European countries (both east and west) lie on profitable through routes but derive no benefits from traffic which originates elsewhere and uses their roads only to deliver elsewhere. Con-

versely, nations on the European coastlines, by the nature of things, originate traffic but have none passing through, except at a few clearly defined ferry ports.

It is an intractable conflict of interests typical of those which add to the friction of European politics, and it is exacerbated by the permits system used by most European governments to control the numbers of foreign vehicles allowed to run in their territories. Sometimes transit by rail is made a condition of permits being granted: this practice is currently favoured by West Germany, while France has for years been trying to get international acceptance of its Kangourou road–rail system. Unfortunately introducing a rail element into a journey inevitably brings with it delays and extra expense, which please neither haulier nor client.

The lack of internationally–sometimes nationally–accepted standards for vehicle dimensions and operating regulations has plagued manufacturers for decades. Some early diesel engines for use in Germany, for example, were made to be readily convertible into petrol burners because a few towns banned diesels after objecting to the exhaust smell. Any firm ambitious to export its vehicles has had to produce quite separate designs for each market, thereby losing many of the economic advantages of volume production. So onerous are these constraints that it has often paid a maker better to withdraw from an overseas sales area rather than become involved in the distractions of trying to cater for it.

One of the most intractable problems for operators trying to keep within the law is the

The world sat up and took notice when Scammell produced the first lorry able to carry 100 tonnes on its back, and that mighty vehicle (left)–which, happily, still survives–opened new horizons to engineers faced with the problems of moving large pieces of electrical and other equipment. That was in 1929, and for a while it seemed nothing bigger could ever be needed. But times continue to change, and 40 years later the size and weight of some consignments was such that it was no longer possible to carry them entirely on wheels without incurring some risk of damage to bridges and other structures. A successful answer was found in applying the principle of the hovercraft: air pumped under the skirts of this giant trailer (below) has the effect of spreading its weight over the whole area, thereby reducing spot loadings to an acceptable level.

A lorry empty weighs less than a lorry laden . . . and in some circumstances it legally needs fewer wheels on the ground when it is empty. So some makers offer means of lifting the trailing axle of a rigid six-wheeler off the ground, thereby reducing tyre scrub, wear, and possibly fuel consumption into the bargain.

apparently straightforward matter of keeping within stipulated weight limits. In those places where weight laws are rigidly enforced they create genuine difficulties. It is perfectly possible for a satisfactory vehicle to be loaded within its overall permitted capacity and with none of its axles overloaded; yet, as it goes about its business making part-deliveries, the effective centre of gravity of the remaining cargo can easily move in such a way as to impose an illegal burden on one axle. This is the main reason why users incur the cost and unladen weight penalty of adding a third trailing axle to a four-wheeler which otherwise appears perfectly able to cope. With some cargoes, gravel for example, a wholly unpredictable weight transfer resulting from the load moving forward during an emergency brake application can easily render driver and owner liable to prosecution. The difficulties for designers and users are inevitably complicated further when articulated vehicles are considered, and confusion becomes worse still when the big modern international containers are involved.

Containerisation for ordinary freight is far from a new or even recent idea: indeed, railwaymen in the 1830s were using box containers or 'lift vans' to tranship from rail wagon to canal and ferry boat, and there was another surge of interest by railways in the 1930s, as they looked for ways to combat the lorry menace. But it was the intercontinental shipping trade 20 years later which created the 'container revolution', adopting rigidly standardised boxes as a means of reducing cargo-handling times, and the expensive and unproductive waiting periods spent by ships tied up at docksides.

But seafaring men view such things as containers from a viewpoint that is very different to the weights-and-dimensions-conscious road haulier, and there can be real difficulties carrying maximum dimension container combinations on lorries that must meet restrictions on overall lengths. More subtle problems arise when a container that has been customs sealed for clearance at an inland port, turns out to have been loaded either excessively or unevenly by consignors who do not have to answer for any overweight infringements on the road-bound parts of the journey, which are perhaps on the far side of the world.

Considerations like braking performance and

lighting are naturally included in the regulations to be observed by the road transport industry, and there have been some determined attempts in recent years to legislate for vehicle performance. The heavily laden and underpowered lorry is generally regarded as a public nuisance and several governments have tried to establish suitable minimum power-to-weight ratios for heavy vehicles. But sheer power is not everything, and over the years self-interest on the part of owners has been more effective than the law in producing satisfactory levels of lorry performance.

The problem of noise is, unfortunately, more intractable: everyone knows how much noise is too much, but hardly anyone can agree on what noises are offensive, and when; the problem is further compounded by the great difficulty in measuring sound in a generally agreed and understandable way. Almost any ordinary diesel-engined lorry can exceed the commonly accepted ideas of reasonable noise levels, and while the main single source of noise is the engine, the problem is underlined by the fact that a large lorry, freewheeling at 50 km/h with its engine turned off, will come perilously near to the acceptable maximum sound levels. Although considerable technical problems result from attempts to silence power units, it can be done; so far, however, quiet-running tyres have eluded designers, as have any effective means of reducing the noise caused by a vehicle moving through the air.

It can be argued that vehicle-produced noise is only a nuisance if there is someone nearby to hear it, so there is a strong lobby that wants lorries kept away from towns and cities, and confined to the purpose-built main roads that cover most countries and continents. This solution well suits lorry owners too, and there is little incentive for commercial vehicles to stray on to narrow crowded roads and pedestrian-congested village streets – except, of course, when deliveries have to be made to the shops and factories that make those towns prosperous. On the whole this problem is less apparent among the newer cities of the world – those laid out and developed during the motor age – than in those places that expanded before the twentieth century. This is another problem with contradictory solutions: adopt the commonly suggested plan for large yards on the outskirts of town, where trainloads (either road or rail) of goods can be transferred to smaller vehicles for the final delivery, and streets would have to accommodate a lot of little trucks rather than fewer large ones. On the other hand, out-of-town hypermarkets and shopping precincts, placed near main motor routes and offering easy access for supplies and customers, are the quickest and surest way of killing off the old inner shopping areas.

Contrary to the fondly-held belief of most vacation-bound passenger car drivers, speeding on their way to snow-covered slopes or the sea, very few modern motor roads were built for their immediate benefit, although a striking virtue of roads over other forms of transport infrastructure is that they are available for use by virtually everyone – a distinct political advantage now that public authorities (which means taxpayers) find themselves financing in one way or another almost every kind of major transport enterprise. By the mid-1920s most nations had ceased to invest in wholesale exten-

sions to their rail systems and were beginning to spend instead on roads: they were bad years, with the great slump beginning to accelerate, and an important incentive for many governments was the pressing need to create work for increasing armies of unemployed labour, and to improve communications with newly developing industrial areas that offered the prospect of new kinds of work in vastly better surroundings. The new roads were extended steadily, their growth encouraged by the increasing reliability of motor vehicles, a desire to open up colonial territories and sometimes – less creditably but ultimately just as useful – with military aims in mind.

During those inter-war years the speeds of motor vehicles, and the dimensions of lorries and buses, were still low enough for traffic and the rest of society to mix without serious harm. Indeed, many a town and small community benefited hugely from the flow of vehicles passing through its shopping area, bringing travellers willing to spend money. But vehicle design and performance, and population, constantly increased at an ever-accelerating rate. By the early 1950s the older-styled mixed traffic motor roads were clearly becoming over-burdened and outclassed, with never-ending streams of traffic ruining towns they had not long before helped to prosperity.

New kinds of road were required, of a kind unknown before; the civil engineering, cost, and disregard for geography and topography was comparable only with the great railway age of a century before. These roads were strictly inter-urban corridors, making no attempt to cater for local needs, but enabling motor journeys undreamed of even half a century before. These new motor roads are invariably planned and built by governments, unlike many of their railway predecessors, and they are seen as main arteries: plenty of extensions are no doubt yet to come, but the essential pattern is already clear and largely complete in most advanced countries. The mere existence of such roads has been sufficient to attract any traffic that could conceivably benefit from using them, and therefore a large measure of lorry routeing occurs naturally without any other spur. Unfortunately, the new roads and the new kinds of traffic they propagate have also encouraged the development of a new kind of heavy vehicle that is even less welcome than its forebears when it has to leave the wide-open spaces of autostrada, freeway, or motorway for the confines of village or city.

The usual reaction to this impasse is an exasperated sigh, and puzzlement about the way our grandparents seemed to manage perfectly well without motor vehicles. But the world has changed so hugely, even since 1950, that there is no way back to the simplicity of yore – populations have increased, and become diffused; incomes and individual expectations have increased even more quickly. Compare (on a basis of price as a proportion of income) the cost of almost every kind of manufactured goods 40 years ago with those of today; look too at the origins of modern-day commodities – buyers now have ready access to a previously unimaginable range of goods and sourcing. And lorries are the catalyst that has done more than anything else to bring it all about.

After the initial push during the years between the World Wars had opened up whole continents to motor traffic, the transport industry settled down to the business of growing up. Following a lull for re-establishment, it became clear after 1945 that new kinds of interurban roads of the kind pioneered by Germany were needed, and another great building programme got under way. Networks of special fast motor roads now cross and link most settled countries and continents.

Many countries found themselves without road networks capable of making use of the newly reliable motor lorry and, like these Americans in the early 1920s, had to set about wholesale construction. Both equipment and methods – and results – were often crude, but this great worldwide effort made possible road transport in the modern sense.

INTO THE FUTURE

It is a wise prophet who avoids committing himself too specifically about what the future is likely to hold, and transport history is liberally decorated with absurd flights of fancy which no doubt seemed sensible enough when they were first postulated. Even with those salutary lessons in mind, however, it is reasonable to make some cautious guesses about the future of commercial road transport – to the end of this century at least, and perhaps even a little beyond that.

First, and most important, it is impossible to foresee any departure from the concept of free-running vehicles on common roads. This principle has held good for thousands of years, and while rival transport modes have occasionally arisen, each has eventually ended up catering only for specific needs. Pipelines, canals, hovercraft and container-carrying airships may well have a place in the order of things, but they are unlikely to impinge seriously upon wheeled road transport at any time in the foreseeable future, for the very good reason that wheels can go almost anywhere while carrying a useful load. Only feet offer greater versatility, but animal traction cannot conceivably provide sufficient speed or capacity for anything more complicated than subsistence economies.

Looking ahead only as far as the year 2000, a great many commentators appear convinced that the world will begin to run seriously short of petroleum early in the new century. Happily, this particular fear seems to be quite unfounded: there is enough oil left for hundreds of years at the present rate of consumption. What certainly will happen during the next quarter-century – indeed, it is beginning to happen now – is that the price of oil-derived products will increase steadily as the easily tapped sources are exhausted and extraction and processing therefore become more difficult; pricing seems likely to become the form of rationing or allocation to which users will become accustomed. Bearing in mind the general usefulness of crude oil in a great many industries, it seems in retrospect particularly unfortunate that so much has simply been burnt. Oil is reckoned to comprise about one per cent of the world's non-renewable energy resources, yet it now comprises something like half of the energy currently consumed.

Commercial road transport is a captive of the oil industry, for liquid fuel is undoubtedly the most convenient and effective way of carrying energy for vehicles, but the vehicle building and operating industries need not be at all ashamed of their progress along the path of fuel efficiency. The historically high cost (price combined with taxes) of fuel has forced designers into a continuous search for economy that has done wonders for engine development and has made it possible for road to challenge rail on a simple tonne (and passenger) per kilometre basis. This is perhaps not so surprising, since many electricity power stations are fuelled by oil and, incidentally, use a great deal more than road transport.

But if the exhaustion of conventional sources of energy is a far from immediate problem, the same cannot be said of the disruption of supplies by political action. This threat is present, permanent and very serious, and it is depressing that more than two decades of such disruptions (ever since the Suez crisis during the mid-1950s) have made no real difference to general energy consumption trends.

Such capricious and in all probability temporary famines of vehicle fuel are more likely to foster a search for alternative sources of oil supply than the development of alternative fuels, but price is another matter: it seems certain that the time is fast approaching when less efficient fuels than those which have served so well during the twentieth century will become economically attractive.

Fortunately, perhaps, there will be no need to look to miniature nuclear plants or solar energy cells for the vehicles of the future: rather, one can look back to what happened in earlier years, because oil has often been in short supply and practicable alternatives were always found. Before the First World War (when the Middle East oilfields were still undeveloped), petrol from Burma and America became expensive in Europe and encouraged considerable experimenting with benzole and alcohol. Benzole, distilled from coal tar, figured large in coal-rich Germany when war cut the country off from petroleum supplies; experimenters in France found success with a half-and-half mixture of alcohol and benzole; at much the same time German chemists found it worthwhile to add napthalene to a similar brew; even now, Australia is producing an acceptable fuel for motor vehicles from brown coal.

Brazil, one of the first countries in more recent times to decide that oil-derived petrol has become too expensive, is currently growing half its vehicle fuel requirements in the form of vegetable matter which is then fermented and distilled into alcohol. Climate obviously plays a major part in deciding

which crops can be grown to the best effect and where, but sugar cane, molasses, sorghum (a sort of millet), cassava and maize have all been found suitable. Unfortunately the result possesses only two-thirds the calorific value of diesel fuel – and, of course, a great deal of space is needed to grow the raw material.

The vegetation, in fact, does not need to be fresh: 60 years ago it was discovered that a ton of peat could be made to yield 110 litres of alcohol. A disconcerting and expensive drawback to alcohol during earlier attempts to popularise its use in motor vehicles was the problem of finding a denaturant making it unpalatable to humans without reducing its calorific value to engines, but modern technology is no doubt capable of finding a solution to that.

An earlier bout of experimenting in Argentina revealed that naptha formed an adequate fuel for more or less standard spark ignition petrol engines. Rather later, during the 1920s and 1930s, when some European nations saw that they might be denied access to oilfields, gas producer engines enjoyed a vogue. The essence of these devices was that steam passed through a bed of incandescent carbon-rich fuel (charcoal or anthracite), the resulting carbon monoxide being an acceptable substitute for petrol. France took the idea seriously, at one stage insisting that in large fleets one lorry in ten must be equipped for producer gas; the Germans were also keen, while Britain, although less enthusiastic, developed some useful designs. The system helped all three nations – and others – extend limited supplies of more conventional fuels during the Second World War.

A regular wartime substitute for petrol in many countries was ordinary coal gas, transported on vehicles in large envelopes at scarcely more than

Despite a great deal of research and money spent over nearly 30 years, it is not likely that gas turbine engines will figure large in road transport. Many makers have tried: Boeing, in collaboration with Kenworth, put a unit into service during the mid-1950s (above). In later years Ford tried another, in the United States and Europe (left). One of the most determined efforts came from Leyland (below), which built a fleet of six gas turbine powered tractors and had them running with ordinary operators.

Most earlier attempts to develop successful producer gas plants sought to mount them on the vehicle itself. When genuine need arose for alternative fuels it was also urgent, and it proved easier to assemble the generators as separate trailer units. Not only were the vehicles themselves kept off the road for a minimum of time, but trailers could be exchanged easily. Such equipment may soon be worth rediscovering.

atmospheric pressure. The whole arrangement was unwieldy and troublesome, and was abandoned as quickly as possible; but stored in high pressure containers of the kind used now for oxygen, acetylene, and other industrial gases, coal gas might well come into its own again. Indeed coal gas, producer gas, and sewage-derived methane have all been used for many years in stationary engines, some of them very large indeed and some driving electricity generators. There is no reason why these gases should not be used more widely in the future, freeing more convenient fuels for vehicle use; indeed, there is nothing at all wrong with washed and compressed sewage gas as a fuel for vehicles.

Another distinctly interesting idea of nearly half a century ago, and now worth reconsidering, was the system pursued with some enthusiasm for a year or two by Herr Erren in Germany. The engines were much like ordinary petrol units – indeed, existing petrol engines were used – but the fuel was hydrogen, carried under high pressure in gas bottles. The potential for future development lay in the source of the fuel, for Erren proposed setting up electrically powered 'cracking' plants that would separate water into its constituent elements, oxygen and hydrogen. Apart from the obvious attractions of an apparently inexhaustable supply of fuel, there is the equally intriguing consideration that, since the cracking can be carried out at any time, the whole process of hydrogen generation becomes, in effect, an alternative to batteries as a means of 'storing' electricity, turning it into a vastly more convenient source of power, and one that would impose none of the crippling limitations of battery-electric vehicles. There has to be a drawback to this attractive scheme of things, of course, and it is both weight and size: to transport an amount of energy equal to the contents of a conventional vehicle fuel tank, a hydrogen reservoir would need to be 20 times bigger and 20 times heavier. No one is likely to be seriously tempted by the difficulties and dangers of using liquid hydrogen.

Early enthusiasts for diesel power were fond of pointing out its alleged ability to consume a wide variety of fuels: indeed, palm, soya and cottonseed oil were all tried sufficiently thoroughly to prove that they would serve, although with a 15 per cent reduction in power compared with ordinary diesel fuel. Groundnut oil, dignified by the grander title of arachide oil, was favoured by Dr Diesel himself – and sounds a better proposition than coal dust, another of the good Doctor's proposals. Short of complete substitution, a sensible and perfectly practicable compromise was to dilute ordinary diesel fuel by up to a third with creosote.

Whatever the causes of petroleum oil famines in the past, however, they have been overcome in one way or another, and conventional fuels always flowed again in quantities and qualities great enough and cheap enough to supersede lesser alternatives.

The oil famines to come are just as likely to hit such matters as lubrication, for the animal and vegetable oils that preceded the modern mineral lubricants left a great deal to be desired, and it may be no easy matter to maintain the standards of long and trouble-free service that users have come to expect from their lubricants. Yet tallow, sperm, rape, coconut, olive and castor oils were once made to serve as engine and machinery lubricants, and it may well be that the enormous reserves of chemical expertise that have accumulated since such endlessly renewable resources were last seriously considered can make them suitable for the future. Shale and tar oils, now too expensive to compete with Persian Gulf and Texan varieties as fuels, will in time become economic feedstocks for lubricants or admixtures to vegetable oils.

The effect of a virtual end, through either scarcity or price, of the oil feedstocks that go to make most modern plastics materials is impossible to predict, but it is comforting to recall that hardly any part of the anatomy of road vehicles can be made only in plastics, and that heavy lorries were built and used long before the plastics era dawned. It would be sad, however, if the remarkable combination of strength, resilience and lightness possessed by the carbon fibre materials now coming into experimental use on heavy vehicles should be denied to designers; but on the whole a shortage of plastics does not seem imminent.

As fuel becomes more expensive there is no doubt that present-day environmental objections to larger lorries will be overruled by other considerations, while at the same time there will be a new impetus towards reducing the unladen weights of all kinds of vehicles. Certainly, there is still some room for further economies in the weight of passenger cars, although superfluous weight is nowadays largely in the form of luxury trimming and styling. It is hard to imagine a much more economic use of space or material than the modern small cars of Europe and Japan, and their makers seem agreed that light alloys are not viable substitutes for steel in mass-producing vehicles.

Somewhat different considerations apply to heavy lorries, and it is noticeable that the unladen weight of recent generations of trucks has shown a marked tendency to increase. One cause is the vastly improved standard of cab comfort and it may be difficult to persuade drivers to give up some of the weighty luxuries that have come their way in recent years. Even so, physically smaller cabs are beginning to evolve from the giant structures of the 1960s, and there seems no good reason why manufacturers' claims to provide passenger car comfort should not be matched by passenger car dimensions, a step that would help considerably in the search for lightness.

A more intractable problem appears to be the considerable weight of high power engines and the transmissions that go with them. Historically the search has been for reliability and power, probably in that order, because vehicle weights and sizes have also increased to offer carrying capacities attractively greater than the weight penalty of the bigger engines needed to haul them. But it seems reasonable to suppose that gross weights for vehicles are now approaching their permanent maxima; there is a general feeling that something in the region of 44 tonnes gross train weight, with 12 tonnes capacity driving axles and engines producing 6bhp/tonne is probably the optimum maximum size of vehicle for all-round efficiency. A few nations already permit such vehicles (or something near to them) and it can only be a matter of time before the internationalism of road transport persuades others to do likewise. In this regard at least, designers are facing a long period of stability during which it should be possible for them to devote to improving the power/weight ratios of their motors the energies that have so far been spent in keeping abreast with changes in legislation.

The great secret weapon of the ordinary reciprocating internal combustion engine in its battles for survival against other forms of motive power has been its still-enormous potential for development. A glance at some now-superseded piston aeroplane engines shows what can be done when considerations other than the usual mundane ones are applied: in less than ten years the power output of the Rolls-Royce Merlin V12 rose from less than 900hp to very nearly 1,800hp. On a more realistic commercial level, several diesel engine makers have proved in their experimental laboratories that a useful service life in road vehicles can be expected from power units basically similar to those now being sold – but producing twice the output.

So engine weight versus power seems to present no major problems for the future; earlier attempts at improving specific output have often centred simply on increasing engine speed by one means or another, but the cycle of events that takes place in diesel engines unfortunately needs time if it is to be performed efficiently, while a highly undesirable side-effect of this approach has often been an unacceptable increase in exhaust emissions resulting from imperfect fuel combustion. Of course, the substitute fuels of the future may not be so antisocial, and spark ignition engines (they could no longer be termed petrol engines) which can run much faster than diesels, may again come into their own for heavy vehicles. A useful side-effect would then become apparent in the campaign to reduce power unit weight: the higher cylinder compressions characteristic of diesels require much stiffer – and heavier – engine components, and it

seems certain that as soon as initial cost ceases to be as important as it is now, the more expensive but lighter metals will come into use, particularly for components such as crankcases and gearbox housings. Indeed, a few manufacturers use them already.

Meanwhile, seekers of greater thermal efficiency (as opposed to simple horsepower) are much interested in American government-sponsored research into a combination engine in which exhaust heat is used to vaporise fluid which turns a turbine before condensing in a closed cycle to be reheated again. By using the turbine output to good account a 15 per cent fuel saving overall is claimed, with the bonus of a 15 per cent reduction in emissions.

While almost anything to do with engine development is at once expensive and time-consuming, quite the opposite is true of air deflectors, which in one guise or another are now saving up to ten per cent of fuel bills for a great many operators. The deflectors are simply shields, moulded in sheet metal or plastics, mounted on the roofs of lorry cabs. They add a measure of 'streamlining' to vehicles which might otherwise have been

Plastics have certainly made their presence felt among the sort of bodywork that is insulated for food transport. Clean contamination-free surfaces are easily obtained and high standards of thermal efficiency are possible. Insulated containers are also used for international container traffic: mobile straddle carriers of this kind are widely used to load and unload lorries.

Above: Opinions differ as to the effectiveness of air deflectors, but user experience shows that appreciable quantities of fuel can be saved when they are intelligently applied. Lorries are not easy things to streamline, but these deflectors, mounted on cab roofs, certainly indicate a useful field for experimenting.

Right: For a few years, when the then-current British Construction and Use regulations encouraged it, the Jensen company used simple airframe techniques to produce full-size vans which, while weighing less than 3 tonnes, could carry 6 tonnes. The underframes were self-supporting, although very light, and built up from standard light alloy sheet and simple sections. It should now be possible to better the Jensen performance of 30 years ago.

designed expressly to create fuel-wasting air turbulence, and they certainly point to a fruitful field for future experiments in improving the lines of cab and body styling.

Many characteristics likely to become apparent in lorries during the next two or three decades are already being tentatively exploited in one form or another. Aluminium alloy chassis frames are used on some weight-conscious American tractors; heavy-duty steels, which can be used appreciably thinner than ordinary kinds, are often specified by European makers. Fabrication techniques continue to improve and can save small but useful amounts of weight. Light alloys could certainly replace steel in a great many components, although the level of performance required of the complete vehicle may well force some major rethinking of traditional forms and functions. Again, the signs are already there: in some vehicle suspension systems, heavy leaf springs have already given way to solid rubber or compressed air (very widely used on full-sized buses and coaches) or simply to much-simplified one-piece steel springs. What is more, none of these modern replacements needs oiling, and all should require less maintenance.

Another area in which there has been steady if

unspectacular progress toward less weight for equivalent or better performance has been that of electrics: once-heavy items like batteries have shed weight and generators are being replaced by much lighter alternators. But it must be admitted that if and when cheap and readily available plastics finally disappear every aspect of the electronics industry will be sorely hit. So, presumably, will the tyre makers, who have tended to forsake natural rubber for other kinds in recent times. Given time, they can no doubt retrace their steps, and it must be hoped that they can continue to offer the standards of reliability that have made it possible for many operators to dispense with (inevitably heavy) spare wheels, and also continue the progress toward smaller and lighter tyres that is already bearing fruit for the owners of some full-size single-decked buses.

Of course, much of this presupposes that the present format of heavy vehicles will remain substantially unchanged for the next quarter of a century, and on the whole it seems likely that not only will a great many of the lorries running in the year 2000 bear a marked resemblance to those of 1980, but their immediate progeny will, too. Everything depends on relative costs: on the point at which the price of our conventional fuels becomes permanently so high that the expense of adapting or changing to substitutes becomes inevitable; and the point at which the higher costs of making and using light alloys and other expensive metals matter less than the disadvantages of heavier steels and cast iron.

So far, however, we have considered only one aspect of road transport, the lorry itself. But developments in quite unrelated fields have already had profound operational effects and are likely to go much further. In communications, the steady progress of telephone services from localised efficiency to international and intercontinental usefulness has already done much to improve the overall effectiveness of a great many industries

One of the few attempts in recent times to make a radical departure from conventional thinking on lorry chassis design was this rear-engined eight-wheeler by Leyland. Unfortunately most users still prefer to buy universal designs – which, by their very universality, are presumably not perfectly matched to every application. But as operating costs continue to rise there may well be sunnier prospects for vehicles designed in every degree for one specific purpose.

Where suitable loads justify the expense it is possible to instal loading and discharging equipment that is positively dramatic in its mode of operation. The trend away from time-wasting and laborious handling has accelerated during the last 20 years or so, and there is no doubt that as transport time becomes ever more valuable, more and more effort will be devoted to efficient cargo handling.

beside transport – and remember that those other industries are themselves users of road transport, and that when they become more efficient so, by association, does the lorry. International telex has also grown rapidly in stature (who would want to go back to the days of telegrams and cables in business?) and is likely to grow a lot more, because in an era of expensive energy there is bound to be a bright future for any means of communication that does not involve physical transference of people and goods.

Road transport will most certainly see a very marked diminution in empty running, and a huge increase in the degree of sophistication applied to finding loads for lorries. Traditionally the efficiency of individual operations, measured on a cost basis, has often involved lorries travelling empty from one delivery to another loading point; in the more rigorous economic climate of the future, there will be big incentives not to consume fuel and time on such unproductive movement. Greater co-ordination of fleets may be one answer, but cargo co-ordination (probably by computer programmes) seems to offer greater scope – coupled, no doubt, with two-way radio links for every vehicle.

It follows that any really useful trend towards 'common user' practices in vehicle operation implies much increased versatility in bodywork, for despite the ease with which a tanker may carry cement or flour, and a tipper coal or sand, it is not easy to see how useful flexibility can go much further. Once again, however, the lines of likely development can already be discerned and it seems safe to assume that the already common articulated vehicle, in which the expensive tractor unit and its driver can haul any compatible semi-trailer, will expand its sphere of influence, as will the interchangeable 'swop body'. Almost inevitable is an extension of double – probably triple – bottom road train operation of the kind already familiar on long hauls in Australia and America, so constructed that the drawbar trailers, each perhaps carrying separate commodities, are readily convertible to semi-trailers for final delivery.

Existing motorised vehicles are certainly well able to haul trailers of considerable capacity; the main hindrances are environmentally sensitive legislatures, which may well find more pressing matters for their attention when the cheap oil finally expires.

Road trains are an obvious way of increasing the quantities of goods moved, without an unreasonable increase in overall operating costs. But such combinations are clearly unsuitable for congested urban roads; it is going to require considerable political will before most countries can bring themselves to spend the money – and energy – that will enable the transport of the future to operate at maximum efficiency.

INDEX